A GUIDE TO

Effective Pastoral Ministry

EDITORS

Steve D. Cassimy

Abraham J. Jules

Nikolaus Satelmajer

Pacific Press® Publishing Association
Nampa, Idaho
Oshawa, Ontario, Canada
www.pacificpress.com

Cover design by Steve Lanto
Inside design by Aaron Troia

Scripture quotations marked NIV are from the HOLY BIBLE, NEW INTER-NATIONAL VERSION®. Copyright © 1973, 1978, 1984 by International Bible Society. Used by permission of Zondervan Publishing House. All rights reserved.

Scriptures quoted from TLB are from *The Living Bible,* copyright © 1971 by Tyndale House Publishers, Wheaton, IL. Used by permission.

Scripture texts credited to NRSV are from the New Revised Standard Version of the Bible, copyright © 1989 by the Division of Christian Education of the National Council of the Churches of Christ in the USA. Used by permission. All rights reserved.

Scriptures quoted from NKJV are from The New King James Version, copyright © 1979, 1980, 1982, Thomas Nelson, Inc., Publishers.

Scriptures quoted from KJV are from the King James Version of the Bible.

The authors assume full responsibility for the accuracy of all facts and quotations as cited in this book.

Adventist® and Seventh-day Adventist® are the registered trademarks of the General Conference Corporation of Seventh-day Adventists®.

ISBN 13: 978-0-8163-2361-6
ISBN 10: 0-8163-2361-5

09 10 11 12 13 • 5 4 3 2 1

Contributing Authors

Jonas Arrais, DMin, is associate secretary of the Seventh-day Adventist Ministerial Association for Elders and editor of the *Elder's Digest* magazine at the Seventh-day Adventist headquarters in Silver Spring, Maryland, U.S.A. Previously, he was associate ministerial secretary for South America and also served as a pastor. He travels the world conducting Elder's Training Sessions and speaks Portuguese, Spanish, and English.

Matthew A. Bediako, MDiv, MSPH, is executive secretary of the worldwide Seventh-day Adventist Church, with headquarters in Silver Spring, Maryland, U.S.A. He served as Bible teacher and chaplain in both Bekwai and Asokoe in Seventh-day Adventist Teacher Training Colleges and president of the Seventh-day Adventist Church in Ghana and in West Africa, and as field secretary and general vice president of the Seventh-day Adventist Church in Silver Spring, Maryland, U.S.A. Bediako has been awarded three Honorary Doctorate degrees. The government and people of Ghana have recently awarded him a "Diplomatic Passport" as recognition of his international activities for humanity.

Steve D. Cassimy, DMin, is ministerial secretary of the Seventh-day Adventist Church in the Greater New York area. His ministry experience includes pastoring in Canada and the United States and he currently serves as a member of the Human Relations Advisory for the church in North America. Cassimy served his community in Scarborough, Ontario, as a chaplain at Centenary Hospital and graduated as a united chaplain in the state of New York. He has traveled throughout the Caribbean Islands, Europe, Africa, Canada, and the United States on speaking engagements. Currently, Cassimy is pursuing a doctoral degree in Pastoral Counseling.

Adrian Craig, BA in Theology, is senior pastor of the Avondale Memorial Seventh-day Adventist Church in Cooranbong, New South Wales, Australia. He has spent seventeen years in pastoral ministry with twelve of those years serving in Papua, New Guinea, with a team to do evangelism and training. He also served as an administrator and a departmental director. Craig believes in the primacy of the Adventist pulpit and maximizing membership participation in mission.

James A. Cress, DMin, serves as the Ministerial Association secretary for the General Conference of Seventh-day Adventists, with headquarters in Silver Spring, Maryland, U.S.A. He testifies that his most satisfactory work was in pastoring local congregations in a variety of locations in the United States, although he also served as evangelist, departmental director, and instructor in evangelistic methods and preaching. Now he testifies that he has the opportunity and privilege, as he travels the world, to encourage and motivate other pastors to excellence in ministry.

Paul Douglas, MBA, CPA, is director of the General Conference Auditing Service (GCAS), located at the Seventh-day Adventist Church headquarters in Silver Spring, Maryland, U.S.A. He serves as the chief audit executive, with a team of more than two hundred professionals operating from offices in forty countries. GCAS performs structurally independent financial audits, reviews of trust operations, and tests of policy compliance for more than twenty-three hundred denominational organizations worldwide.

Karnik Doukmetzian, LLB, is general counsel of the world headquarters of the Seventh-day Adventist Church in Silver Spring, Maryland, U.S.A. Previously he was vice-president of Adventist Risk Management, Inc. After practicing law in Ontario, Canada, for a number of years, he served as general counsel, trust services, and religious liberty director for the Seventh-day Adventist Church in Canada. Doukmetzian has the license to practice law in the United States and Canada. He is a member of the American Bar Association, Canadian Bar Association, Tennessee Bar Association, Law Society of Upper Canada, and the Defense Research Institute.

R. Clifford Jones, DMin, PhD, is associate dean and professor in the Christian Ministry Department of Andrews University, Berrien Springs, Michigan, U.S.A. Prior to joining the University faculty, he pastored churches in the northeastern part of the United States including two African American congregations in New York City. He has authored numerous articles in professional and scholarly journals and two books. He enjoys interacting with students, hearing their stories, tuning into their journeys and helping them achieve their goals.

Abraham Julius Jules, DMin, is pastor of the Mt. Vernon Seventh-day Adventist Church in Mt. Vernon, New York, U.S.A. Previously, Jules was the pastor of several churches in New York City and has been the featured speaker at numerous revivals, weeks of prayer, workers' meetings, camp meetings, and seminars in evangelism and church administration throughout the world. He has also held many evangelistic meetings. Jules is the speaker of the television program, *Pathway of Hope,* which can be seen twice weekly on Hope TV, a Seventh-day Adventist television network.

D. Robert Kennedy, PhD, is senior pastor of the Seventh-day Adventist Church of the Oranges in Northern New Jersey. He has spent time as a college theology professor, administrator, and departmental leadership. During his current pastoring experience, he testifies that he is testing his theoretical understanding of theology and leadership. He has written several articles for journals and magazines, has published six books, contributed to others, and prepared several manuals for the academic and practical areas that have been most helpful to students, pastors, and local church leaders. He and his wife, Dr. S. June Kennedy, present Parental Legacy seminars and other topics in various settings.

Alvin Maurice Kibble, MDiv, STM, is a vice president at the North American headquarters of the Seventh-day Adventist Church, located at Silver Spring, Maryland, U.S.A., and chairs committees and serves with a variety of Adventist service organizations. Previously, he was president of the Allegheny East area of Seventh-day Adventist churches and pastored churches in Maryland, New York, New Jersey, Virginia, and Pennsylvania. He has also conducted evangelistic meetings and revivals throughout the United States, Bermuda, England, Jamaica, and Africa.

Robert Kyte, JD, was general counsel of the Seventh-day Adventist Church with headquarters in Silver Spring, Maryland, U.S.A., with involvement in general corporate matters, commercial transactions, general nonprofit law, and intellectual property. He is now general counsel for Healthwise, Incorporated. Before joining the office of General Counsel, Kyte was a member of a law firm in Boise, Idaho, with a practice that included corporate law, commercial transactions, general nonprofit law, municipal financing, and estate planning. He also served as president and general counsel for Pacific Press® Publishing Association.

Pardon K. Mwansa, DMin, is a general vice president of the Seventh-day Adventist Church, with headquarters in Silver Spring, Maryland, U.S.A. Previous to his current assignment, he was president of the Southern Africa-Indian Ocean area of the Seventh-day Adventist Church. Besides serving as pastor in a variety of positions such as administrative, he also became the associate stewardship director of the General Conference of Seventh-day Adventists. Mwansa was a television speaker for the Gospel Penetration Ministries in Zambia.

John S. Nixon, DMin, is senior pastor for the Collegedale Seventh-day Adventist Church on the campus of Southern Adventist University in Collegedale, Tennessee. He has served in parish ministry, primarily in urban areas and college campuses, including New York City; Boston, Massachusetts; Los Angeles, California; and Washington, D.C. He also served in an administrative position in southern California for the Seventh-day Adventist Church.

Chek Yat Phoon, PhD, is education director at the church headquarters in the Northern Asia Pacific area in South Korea. He has rich experiences in pastoral, theological, educational, counseling, and administrative leadership. His degree from Andrews University in Religious Education concentrated on Pastoral Counseling. He also served as Ministerial Association secretary, Adventist Chaplaincy Ministries, Family Ministry director, and Leadership Education and Development coordinator for the Southeast Asia Union Mission in the Southern Asia-Pacific Division.

Sally Lam-Phoon, PhD, is director for Children's, Family, and Women's Ministries and Shepherdess coordinator. Previously, she was professor and academic dean of Hong Kong Adventist College and has been working as Education and Women's Ministries director at the South Asia Union Mission. As a pastoral team, she and her husband, Chek Yat Phoon, have conducted numerous seminars for ministerial couples all over Asia with the aim of helping them discover and maximize their potential. Both were associated with Southeast Asia Union College in Singapore and later at Hong Kong Adventist College in classroom and administrative levels.

Leslie N. Pollard, PhD, DMin, is vice president for Loma Linda University Adventist Health Sciences Center, located in Loma Linda, California, U.S.A. He leads diversity education, promotion, recruitment, and retention for the University. Pollard began his leadership career in southern California as a parish minister and has served as youth pastor, chaplain, college teacher, and educational and healthcare administrator. He has served as an international leadership trainer and teacher around the world. Pollard has published many articles in journals, is a guest columnist for the *Adventist Review,* and recently authored a book entitled *Embracing Diversity: How to Reach People of All Cultures* that has been translated into Spanish, French, and German.

Juan R. Prestol, MBA, is undertreasurer of the General Conference of Seventh-day Adventists, with headquarters in Silver Spring, Maryland, U.S.A. Previous to this appointment, his career history includes being treasurer of the Seventh-day Adventist Church in North America, Euro-Asia Division, Atlantic states, and Bermuda. He began his denominational work in Dominica. He graduated with a major in Business Administration and a minor in Religion from Andrews University and plans to graduate from Andrews University in 2009 with a PhD in Management.

Ángel Manuel Rodríguez, ThD, is director of the Biblical Research Institute at the Seventh-day Adventist world headquarters and a member of the American Society of Biblical Literature and the American Academy of Religion. He has served as president of Antillian Adventist University and academic vice president of Southwestern Adventist University, authored several books, and writes a monthly column for *Adventist World.* He has lectured on a variety of theological topics to ministers and lay groups around the world.

Nikolaus Satelmajer, DMin, is editor of *Ministry,* located at the Seventh-day Adventist Church headquarters in Silver Spring, Maryland, U.S.A. He also serves as associate ministerial secretary and conducts workshops for ministers and members, speaks at camp meetings and educational institutions, and has coordinated numerous Professional Growth seminars for ministers of all denominations. He also conducts evangelistic meetings worldwide and has pastored churches and worked as an administrator in the United States and Canada. He is currently working on a STM degree in historical theology.

Benjamin D. Schoun, DMin, is president of Adventist World Radio, the worldwide mission radio arm for the Seventh-day Adventist Church, located in Silver Spring, Maryland, U.S.A. He also serves as a general field secretary of the General Conference of Seventh-day Adventists. Prior to this appointment, he was president of the church in the Atlantic states and northern New England. He also served as a professor, program director, and associate dean at the Seventh-day Adventist Theological Seminary, located at Andrews University in Berrien Springs, Michigan, U.S.A., as well as a pastor and youth director. His publications include a book entitled *Helping Pastors Cope* and a number of articles in a variety of publications.

Walton (Walt) A. Williams, DMin, is an associate ministerial secretary for the Seventh-day Adventist Church in North America, with headquarters in Silver Spring, Maryland, U.S.A. He is on assignment to the Seventh-day Adventist Theological Seminary, located in Berrien Springs, Michigan, U.S.A., which coordinates the seminary's North American field-delivery of the master's degree in Pastoral Ministry, as well as the first two years of an innovative Master of Divinity option. His excitement for InMinistry is driven by his passion for equipping young pastors by facilitating work-embedded adult learning techniques. His service record also includes administration positions in the Montana area and in Georgia, U.S.A.

Contents

Preface

Can you imagine over twenty individuals—ministers, church leaders, administrators, and financial specialists—who have pledged their lives to congregational ministry, writing chapters in a book focusing on the latest and best methods for ministry? We might call *A Guide to Effective Pastoral Ministry* a landmark publication that will inspire those who wish to make a significant difference in the lives of their parishioners as they function in the role of a pastor. This book, the most comprehensive book ever published in the Seventh-day Adventist denomination on pastoral ministry, covers a broad range of topics featuring various aspects of ministry that we believe will be exceptionally useful to our ministers around the world.

To proclaim the gospel of Jesus Christ certainly challenges those in pastoral ministry. Our leadership of congregations has, of necessity, changed both in scope and responsibility. The authors of this book recognize the variety of tasks that congregational ministers, in particular, face. And, as pastors endeavor to meet the needs of every ethnic group, all of whom have various experiences and backgrounds, the necessity for suggestions and inspiration increases. Therefore, the authors of this book have attempted to cover some of the challenges that pastors encounter in the different parts of the world. Glancing at the chapter titles, "The Pastor as a Person," "The Pastor as a Shepherd," "The Pastor as Worship

Leader," for instance, each reader will gain a quick concept of the expanse and value of each section.

As we revisit our history and see how this church has traversed the continents of the world from the smallest beginning, we recognize a specific need to be able to relate our mission to various segments of the world field in relevance and practicality. When we scan the biographies of the authors of the various chapters, we see a dynamic of experience as devoted ministers have allowed the Holy Spirit to experiment, to mentor, and to model the example of Christ in displaying full commitment and sacrifice.

This book does not merely record theoretical instruction, but declares that we've been there and attempted, through the Holy Spirit's power, to reach individuals in every area of the world. To all those in Christ's service around the world, I ask you to please read this book. Digest it. Pray for the Holy Spirit to imbue your mind as you comprehend the various topics discussed. We are living in an age of great complexity, and, therefore, we need all the help we can get. We consider the calling to the ministry as the most serious and profound calling, and we recognize the need for unity of purpose for pastors. Although this book will not fulfill a mechanical application to ministry, the Holy Spirit will use your absorption of these pages to speak to your heart as you apply this material to your various venues.

Written by individuals who have extensive ministry experience, as well as expertise in other kinds of ministry, this publication features several who have not had ministerial experience, but who have been working closely with ministers in the fulfillment of the gospel commission. Thus, these individuals not only write from what they have studied but also by what they have experienced in the areas in which they have gained recognition.

As I commend this book to our ministerial colleagues around the world, I know that they will not only be blessed but will have an opportunity to improve their ministerial skills. Also, I commend this book to students studying for ministry as they anticipate the privilege of serving as a Seventh-day Adventist minister and prepare for the challenges that will come their way. I thank the Lord Jesus Christ that He has called us to be the Seventh-day Adventist Church and that He has called us as ministers of this denomination.

Matthew A. Bediako, secretary
General Conference of Seventh-day Adventists

Introduction

Bringing together, in book form, a number of distinguished pastors and denominational leaders from around the world to share their experiences and wisdom with the rest of the Seventh-day Adventist clergy was a concept conceived by the three editors. In consultation with Dr. James A. Cress, ministerial secretary of the world church, we selected authors from around the world who would contribute chapters in specific areas of ministry in which writers have distinguished themselves.

This was certainly not an easy assignment given the fact that many individuals in Seventh-day Adventist ministry could have been chosen. However, we are extremely pleased with the final group of writers who have given their input to this project.

In many ways, this book will serve as an incentive to those in ministry to pursue excellence. The chapter content holds the potential to further enhance one's ability to not only experience periodic success but to maintain a vibrant ministry and encourage others during difficult and seemingly fruitless days of service.

Because we interacted with fellow ministers from around the world, we now understand more of the common experiences we share, and also recognize that we see and sometimes experience the same things differently. This was a very enlightening and positive experience.

Abraham Jules wishes to thank his wife, Dominique, and daughter,

Cheyenne, for their undying love and support. Steve Cassimy wishes to thank his wife, Marilyn, who has been a source of strength during this exercise, daughter Lavona, sister Sonia Rodney-Williams, and administrative assistant Prudence Chase for their technical help in preparing the document. Nikolaus Satelmajer thanks his wife, Ruth, who was doing extra duties at home, so that he could devote more time to the project. He also thanks Myrna Tetz for doing quality editing and Sheryl Beck, editorial specialist of *Ministry,* for coordinating the flow of the manuscript.

We extend a thank you to all our contributors for their time and effort in making this project a reality. We believe that this book will be a treasure of wisdom and encouragement for all who are engaged in the proclamation of the gospel in these tumultuous times in which we live.

Steve D. Cassimy
Abraham J. Jules
Nikolaus Satelmajer

Chapter 1

The Pastor as a Person

Chek Yat Phoon and Sally Lam-Phoon

Flashing on the screen were video shots of highly successful pastors and Christian leaders standing tall amid thunderous applause as hundreds upon hundreds, sometimes even thousands of sinners came to repentance, the result of their work. Yet, we could not quite figure out the glee and delight of all that were gathered as each report was given, as hundreds responded to Pastor Mack's call. Yes, he had been riding on success upon success, having stayed on the road for months away from family doing God's work. Pastor Khoo stood proudly by the large group of candidates he had prepared for baptism—obviously on an emotional high. You could see how the young people adored him as he taught them, played with them, and tended to their needs.

Lucifer was chuckling to himself, pleased at the results of his most successful tactic—one that his evil mind had personally designed—and what we call "Operation Outside In" (in contrast with the gospel that flows from the inside out). Lucifer aims this technique at gifted and earnest individuals who are willing and happy to be involved in the service of God. Lucifer knew that instead of going counter to what Christian leadership stood for, a much more effective strategy was to encourage them to do so much good and savor so much success that it became the driving force for their ministry. His idea was to get them so hooked to *doing* that they forgot about their *being*.

19

You see, while Pastor Mack was enjoying his ministry, his wife was suffering from depression as she struggled to attend to two young children and an ailing mother while attempting to work part time. Because she was a pastor's wife, she kept her disillusionment close to herself; no one saw her tears while she tried to appear cheerful in front of her mother.

Mrs. Khoo had been worried for the health of her pastor-husband for years now. While there was no doubt as to how successful Pastor Khoo had been in the last few years, it had taken a toll on his health, for he was physically drained. The black rings around his eyes bore testimony to inadequate rest and sleep. The Khoos had experienced many disagreements over his working, eating, and sleeping habits. This had inevitably strained their relationship to a point that Mrs. Khoo was seriously contemplating leaving her husband but had hesitated time and time again because of his vocation. Her unhappiness was quite obvious to the parishioners, and many had been critical of her apparent control over her much-loved husband whom they thoroughly enjoyed.

Besides the pastor's health problems, their eleven-year-old son, Ming, was slipping into bad company and experimenting with drugs and alcohol. Even though he had very little time for his own children, no amount of pleading changed the inordinate amount of energy that Pastor Khoo used in his ministry, always tending to some need among his members.

The tug-of-war that takes place in the lives of pastors between their personal and public lives often creates dilemmas that eat into the very soul. These slips and falls in the lives of ministers call our attention to pastors as persons, fallible human beings just like the parishioners they serve. While they have been called by God to serve His people, pastors should always remember that they are not angels nor are they God. As sin-prone individuals, they have to walk a tightrope and maintain balance in a number of areas in their personal lives, such as personal growth and sanctification, balancing the being and the doing, and prioritizing family in relationship with work.

1. Personal growth and sanctification. Pastors should recognize that they are first Christians before they are ministers. As Christians, they need to fully depend upon God, daily seeking His will and drawing strength from His Word. Thus, they must seek Christian growth on a daily basis, understanding sanctification as the work of a lifetime.

While one cannot overemphasize the importance of the personal Christian growth of ministers, this growth cannot be achieved by the accumulation of theology degrees or by the constant search for more knowledge. How often we have watched those highly qualified individuals feel that they know so much more than those whom they serve that they do not need to study the Scriptures anymore.

Henry and Richard Blackaby put it this way: "Leaders in full-time Christian ministry . . . are busy people. . . . The danger for them to neglect their time with God is more subtle, because their Bibles are open so often for sermon preparation, counseling, and other religious work. If they aren't careful, they'll view their Bibles as a textbook rather than as the living Word of God. They'll begin substituting their public prayer life for their personal conversations with God."[1]

Growth does not come by hard work either, but rather, as the result of an imperceptible transformation of lives through grace as pastors daily learn to be still with the open Word of God, allowing God to teach them, to reprove and rebuke them. The Spirit will show them where they need to change and improve; He will point out their secret sins and motivate them to ask forgiveness and strength to overcome. As they learn to tune their ears to His Word and His voice, one-on-one He will prompt them as to where He works so they can join Him in the harvest of souls.

Peter wrote, "But grow in the grace and knowledge of our Lord and Savior Jesus Christ" (2 Peter 3:18, NIV). Ellen White says that grace "was sent in search of us"[2] and God abundantly provides this grace that "we may accomplish everything that [He] requires."[3] Philippians 1:6 emphasizes, "I am sure that God who began the good work within you will keep right on helping you grow in his grace until his task within you is finally finished on that day when Jesus Christ returns" (TLB).

Hence, this growth process will never be completed until Jesus comes. No wonder Ellen White says that Christian growth or sanctification is the work of a lifetime.[4] As long as Satan reigns, we will have self to subdue, sins to overcome, with no possibility of anyone saying, "I have finally arrived at maturity."

For their part, pastors must, on a daily basis, connect with the Word of God, study it, and use it as a guide in deciding on their highest goals and which of those are deemed best for God's kingdom and for His glory.

2. Balancing between being and doing. The work of the gospel must flow from the inside out in contrast to Satan's "Operation Outside In." Their motivation for doing has to come from a quiet sense of being engrafted to the Vine so that what they do stays God-focused. This comes not from anything external, such as good results often termed success or self-fulfillment, but rather by doing God's will, even when they don't receive the applause of men or a pat on the back.

However, this does not mean that when ministry does not draw individuals closer to Christ, pastors have the perfect excuse. God has promised that all who are engrafted to the Vine will bear fruit and enjoy an abundant harvest. He has also promised prosperity and blessings to those who obey Him and follow His bidding.

A state of being in Christ will provide the motivation to witness and then create a sense of urgency to share the gospel to a dying world. Unless pastors consciously recognize the fine balance between being and doing, they may fall into the traps of overdoing or underdoing.

In the case of overdoing, pastors often run into the common pitfall of burnout. When this happens, they may wonder why the passion for ministry has disappeared and begin to doubt if they have been truly called.

In his book *Clergy Self-Care: Finding a Balance for Effective Ministry,* Roy M. Oswald quotes Robert Sabath: "Burnout holds the potential for making us either cynics or saints. In the midst of burnout, we have a choice. We can swing from the heights of all our unmet expectations to the detached withdrawal of no expectations at all. Or we can learn to grow in faith and transfer our misplaced expectations to the proper focus in God alone."[5]

Burnout results in spiritual battles because pastors become too involved in *doing* and neglect the *being* aspect. However, burnout can have a positive side when this experience points them to rely on the grace of God and realize their own human limitations. It can lead pastors to "greater wholeness" and a call to "a commitment to a healthier balance in ministry."[6]

One cannot overemphasize the fact that pastors as persons should be consciously protective of their emotional and physical health. Following the laws of good health in eating right, exercising regularly, getting enough rest, drinking enough water, enjoying the sunshine and fresh air, and demonstrating temperance and an implicit trust in God are essential to physical wholeness. In addition, pastors also need to find emotional support in a confidante, a fellow traveler who can act as a sounding board and counselor in times when the going gets rough.

While on one hand, many pastors overwork and suffer burnout, some are guilty of ministerial laziness. Adolph Bedsole said, "The pastor has a better opportunity to be lazy for a longer period of time without his laziness being discovered than any other person in the community. A lazy pastor is like a porcupine; he may have a lot of fine points, but he will ultimately come to want for company. We preachers bring many of our heartaches upon ourselves by unadulterated laziness."[7]

Finding the fine balance between being and doing requires wisdom from the Holy Spirit. Yes, it is true that when pastors are engrafted to the Vine, they can rest assured that God will accomplish what He wills through them without striving through human effort alone. But this does not mean that they won't have to exert any effort, for it calls for due diligence on their part as well. In the book *Education* is found this beautiful verse:

> "The heights by great men reached and kept
>   Were not attained by sudden flight,
> But they, while their companions slept,
>   Were toiling upward in the night."[8]

A final aspect of being can be found in introspection and self-evaluation. At evaluations by mentors and leaders, pastors need to reflect on how they could improve. In cases where an absence of evaluation exists, perhaps the pastor could be proactive in requesting an evaluation from their supervisors.

In the busy life of a pastor, seeking first to be healthy spiritually, physically, and emotionally is the key to wholeness. This state of health will enable pastors to look at themselves candidly, without the element of selfish pride, to admit their weaknesses and rejoice in their strengths that grace has accorded them. Then, a willingness to adjust where adjustments are called for is paramount to the growth process.

3. Prioritizing family in relationship to work. During a pre-ordination interview, a candidate was asked how he would rank in order the following with regards to priority of service: God, church, and family. The answer came loud and clear for *God*. Then he hesitated, "Church and family, which should be next?" After a couple of moments, the candidate said, "Family should be second, then church." Why the hesitation? Having the right answer is not as important as living life with priorities that often reflects on the value system we hold dear.

In no uncertain terms, Ellen G. White declares, "One well-ordered, well-disciplined family tells more in behalf of Christianity than all the sermons that can be preached. Such a family gives evidence that the parents have been successful in following God's directions, and that their children will serve Him in the church....

"The greatest evidence of the power of Christianity that can be presented to the world is a well-ordered, well-disciplined family. This will recommend the truth as nothing else can, for it is a living witness of its practical power upon the heart."[9]

One area of the pastor's personal life that can remain well hidden for a long time or may never be discovered by their church, centers around family relationships. We know of a pastor who was not only a spiritual leader but a well-published author and speaker, apparently casting a positive influence far and wide, while his own marriage was in shambles. His patient and supportive wife, although bleeding inside from years of emotional abuse and neglect, kept her sorrow all to herself until their children were grown, before seeking healing for herself in another country.

In the book *Suzanne's Diary for Nicholas*,[10] James Peterson likens living to juggling five different balls—work, family, friends, health, and integrity. Work, as the first ball and often the entire focus for many, is made of rubber. If you drop the ball on work, it will bounce right back. However, the other four balls are made of fragile glass. Once dropped, they will never be the same again.

With such an overemphasis on "carrying the rubber ball" (doing the Lord's work), pastors often don't even think twice when they drop the family ball again and again.

Henry and Richard Blackaby cited the following incident about Theodore Roosevelt in his role as president of the United States and as a father to his daughter, Alice. When asked by a friend why he was unable to take an active role in supervising his free-spirited daughter, Alice, he replied, "I can be president of the United States, or I can attend to Alice. I can't do both."[11] To President Roosevelt, his priority was his country. Although he might be able to get away with a statement like this, pastors cannot afford to set their family aside in preference to work.

The Bible gives us this clear injunction regarding bishops and poses a powerful rhetorical question. "The saying is sure: whoever aspires to the office of bishop desires a noble task. Now a bishop must be above reproach, married only once, temperate, sensible, respectable, hospitable, an apt teacher, not a drunkard, not violent but gentle, not quarrelsome, and not a lover of money. He must manage his own household well, keeping his children submissive and respectful in every way—for *if someone does not know how to manage his own household, how can he take care of God's church?*" (1 Timothy 3:1–5, NRSV; italics supplied).

Not just one of the aspects of the personhood of a pastor, a strong pastoral family lies at the very core of ministry. Salvation has to begin with the pastor's own family, with their influence moving from the inside out. Perhaps the greatest challenge lies in pastoring the home flock because at home pastors often hang loose, take off their masks, and are able to be their real selves. Home often becomes an environment where tempers flare and words cut as the tensions gathered from the pastor's work among unreasonable and demanding people are released. Pastors may not even think twice about showing their ugly side because they are away from the public eye. Hence, pastors need to be reminded that one of the greatest contributions they can make to God's kingdom is to nurture their own families as a testimony to the power of God in loving relationships.

After all, what is the point if pastors can win the world for Jesus but their family members end up being lost? How will pastors answer God at His coming when He asks, "Where is your flock—the family flock that I have entrusted you with?"

Gary Chapman[12] shares five indicators of a loving family that may be couched in the following questions for pastors, in order to assess the status of their relationship with family:

1. Do family members exhibit an attitude of service?
2. Is there intimacy between the pastor and his or her spouse?
3. Do the parents teach and train the children?
4. Do children obey and honor the parents?
5. Are pastors loving spouses as well as loving leaders in the home?

Although the ministry is a calling, it should never control us and our plans for marriage and family enrichment. Pastors should live what they preach; they should be models of the spiritual and moral values first in the home and then in the church.

Grace works from the inside out, first to save pastors and then to grow pastors. So long as they submit to a daily relationship with God through His Word and constant communion with Him through prayer, He will keep them on this inside-out track as His Spirit works in them. When they neglect this connection, they go down the slippery slope and find themselves operating from the outside in, where the love for people's applause and the subtle draw of affirmation and recognition become the driving force as they work towards self-glory.

In *Ministry* magazine, E. E. Cleveland penned these words:

The Minister

I am a minister—the face of the church—the voice for God.
Men see in me the gospel preached—and lived,
The path the Master trod—the law fulfilled.

And if somehow I fail to stand the test,
Then in men's eyes God, too, has failed.
The guilt on all the ministry doth rest,
And to His cross our Lord again is nailed.[13]

1. Henry and Richard Blackaby, *Spiritual Leadership* (Nashville, TN: Broadman & Holman Publishers, 2001), 250.

2. Ellen G. White, *The Ministry of Healing* (Mountain View, CA: Pacific Press® Publishing Association, 1942), 161.

3. Ellen G. White, *Christ's Object Lessons* (Washington, DC: Review and Herald® Publishing Association, 1941), 301.

4. Ellen G. White, *The Acts of the Apostles* (Mountain View, CA: Pacific Press® Publishing Association, 1911), 560.

5. Roy M. Oswald, *Clergy Self-Care: Finding a Balance for Effective Ministry* (Bethesda, MD: The Alban Institute, 1991), 75.

6. Ibid., 74, 75.

7. Adolph Bedsole, *The Pastor in Profile* (Grand Rapids, MI: Baker Book House, 1958), 71.

8. Ellen G. White, *Education* (Mountain View, CA: Pacific Press® Publishing Association, 1903), 296.

9. Ellen G. White, *The Adventist Home* (Nashville, TN: Southern Publishing Association, 1952), 32.

10. James Peterson, *Suzanne's Diary for Nicholas* (Great Britain: Headline Book Publishing, 2001), 24.

11. Henry and Richard Blackaby, *Spiritual Leadership,* 252.

12. Gary Chapman, *Five Signs of a Loving Family* (Manila, Philippines: OMF Literature Inc., 1999), contents page.

13. E. E. Cleveland, "The Minister," *The Ministry,* September 1969, 38.

Chapter 2

The Pastor and Theology

Ángel Manuel Rodríguez

Introduction

Although the terms *theology* and *theologian* were used in non-Christian Greek literature, they apparently were intentionally avoided by the biblical writers. In Greek usage, a theologian was a person who spoke of the gods or about divine things,[1] using mythological discourse. During the first two centuries, the Christian church did not have theologians, and yet much theology was formulated by the church. Early in the second century A.D., the term *theology* was being employed to designate the expression of the Christian faith.[2] In the Middle Ages, a theologian described a person professionally dedicated to the study and teaching of theology.[3] That understanding of the term continues to be the prevailing one in the Christian world. Christian theology has become an academic discipline and a theologian a well-trained academician. The vastness of the field of theology gave rise to specializations such as biblical theology, historical theology, systematic theology, pastoral theology, etc.

Today it is practically impossible to provide a definition of theology acceptable to all. Here we can only provide a working definition that will help us in our discussion on the relationship between the pastoral work and the theological task. We suggest that for our purpose, we identify theology as the study of the nature and work of God as He has revealed Himself to us in an attempt to better understand the world and ourselves. In that sense, then, theologians are individuals who reflect on the God they worship, on what He has done and is doing for them, and on the nature of a proper response to Him. Therefore, every believer becomes, in a nontechnical sense, a theologian.[4]

Ministry and theology—inseparable

As indicated above, in the apostolic church, there were not theologians in academic settings as we understand the term today. The role of understanding the Christian message, teaching and proclaiming it, and developing its meaning and significance, was in the hands of the apostles, pastors, and teachers in the church. The doing of theology was at the service of the church with its ministry of reconciliation (cf. 2 Corinthians 5:17–21). In fact, asking at that time whether the pastor was a theologian or not would have been inconceivable. The connection between ministry and theology is still maintained at least in the training of ministers.

The ministerial curriculum contains, among many other things, two general fundamental components, namely methods and content. Courses dealing with method have to do with how to perform the work of the ministry. They deal with matters of church administration, evangelism, homiletics, and counseling, for example, and seek to enable the future ministers to function effectively in the performance of their responsibilities. Content courses provide the fundamental knowledge related to the nature, role, and significance of the ministry. Here theology plays a central role in the formation of pastors by exposing them to the different branches of theology (e.g., biblical theology, systematic theology, and pastoral theology). This aspect of the curriculum does not pretend to form theologians in the technical sense of the term, but provides for future ministers the basic tools that will enable them to function as theologians in the execution of their ministry in the setting of the local parish. It will also enable them to speak intelligently about theological matters and to develop their theological skills through further formal academic studies or as an autodidact through readings and dialogue with trained theologians.

Although we have separated method from theology, the separation is artificial. In other words, theology cannot be separated from the ministerial labor. How ministers perform their work can be determined by their biblical ecclesiology and more particularly by their theology of the ministry. Therefore, ministers will always examine the theological and doctrinal foundation as well as the impact of what they are planning to do or accomplish in the parish.[5] The *how* needs to be evaluated by the content of the gospel they have been called to proclaim. With everything they do determined by their understanding of God in His self-revelation in Christ, preserved for us in the Scriptures, they seek to do His will for them and for the church. This equates with theology in its deepest and more dynamic sense.

Theological function of pastors

The relationship between pastors and theology does not abruptly end after they leave the seminary. The interaction should continue throughout their ministerial work, in order to have a more effective ministry. Based on the previous remarks, we can now proceed to explore in more detail the specific roles of ministers as theologians in their own right.

1. Ministry and theology: Missiological interaction. While theological tasks within the church should be constantly oriented toward the mission of the church, the same applies to the pastoral work. Ministry, by its very nature, is mission oriented. Pastors are in mission as they serve the needs of the congregation, as well as when they reach out to the community as ambassadors for Christ. Within this context, it needs to be reaffirmed that mission and message are an indivisible unity, and that consequently theological thinking includes an intrinsic part of the missiology of the church (cf. Matthew 8:18–20). The nature of the Christian ministry reminds theologians in the academe that when theology is out of touch with the reality of the church, its mission, and its needs, it could be damaging or even useless. Theology has to be motivated by ministry or it cannot be called Christian theology.[6] Pastors do this type of theology constantly—a theology encrusted in mission and that, like all true theology, challenges the mind and dynamically integrates into the life of the church.

But this understanding of theology, as inseparable from mission and message, places serious demands on the pastor for an effective ministry and equates with a theologically well-informed ministry. In order to perform the mission of the church, pastors will need a clear comprehension of the message they intend to proclaim. Uncertainty with respect to the theological content of what we need to proclaim and teach reveals itself in a lack of personal commitment and theological and doctrinal ambivalence (cf. Hebrews 2:1). The pulpit becomes a stage from which the public is entertained and from which the power of the gospel to change lives and to move the hearers to a commitment to Christ and the message and mission of His church is absent—an inherent danger. This absence of true biblical theology from the pulpit betrays the mission and message of the church. Pastors as theologians need to have a clear understanding of the message and mission of the church, in order to fulfill their divine call to the ministry. In the performance of that task, they will model the true nature of theology to professional theologians within the church who may have forgotten it.

2. Ministry and theology: A common search for meaning. The theological task demands from the theologian a spirit of inquisitiveness, a constant desire to gain a deeper comprehension of the message of salvation.[7] But this search for the apprehension of the knowledge of God revealed in the life, work, and ministry of Christ does not remain as the exclusive property of theologians. The nature of the Christian experience includes seeking a deeper understanding of the gospel of salvation. This theological concern appears to have been placed by God in the heart of every believer, and must be satisfied and nurtured not only through personal devotion but particularly through the ecclesiastical ministry. In that task, theologians and pastors work together. With no topic deeper than the redemptive work of Christ on our behalf, every Christian should explore its significance and experiential power. Paul says, "And I pray that you, being rooted and established in love, may have power, together with all the saints, to grasp how wide and long and high and deep is the love of Christ, and to know this love that surpasses knowledge" (Ephesians 3:17b–19a, NIV). The knowledge Paul describes here is more than intellectual; it reaches deep into the human soul and transforms it.

Like the theologian, ministers study and explore the Word to expand their knowledge and clarify and apply it to the life of the community of faith. The only possible difference may be that professional theologians flesh out the result of their studies in the language of theological discourse, making it difficult for church members to comprehend their conclusions. Not that theologians intentionally complicate the simple, but rather, in the search for precision of expression, technical terminology becomes extremely useful. This makes the role of pastors as theologians of particular importance as they minister to those who also want to comprehend better the faith they hold as true.

Pastors then function as mediators of theological knowledge to their congregations. Their acquaintance with theological discourse enables them to filter out the complexity of theological expression, in order to articulate the message in the common language of the parishioners. In other words, pastors stand between the trained theologian and the untrained church member to find ways to make the deep truths of the Scripture intelligible to those they minister.[8] This theological aspect of the ministry does not only contribute to make relevant the biblical message but also to nurture and develop the cognitive and religious experiences of the saints.

3. Ministry and theology: Apologetical task. The history of Christian theology reveals that one of several basic functions of the theological enterprise includes the articulation of the Christian faith in a relevant and persuasive form within the society in which the church procures to fulfill its mission. In the realization of that important responsibility, theologians often become apologists of the Christian gospel. Christianity constantly competes with many other religious and philosophical ways of thinking and life that are essentially incompatible with each other. Demonstrating the correctness, logic, and experiential significance of the gospel in the life of the individual requires persuasive arguments and good communication skills. Apologetics have played an important role in the history of Christianity and particularly in the theological arena.

Pastors fulfill the theological task by proclaiming and defending the faith that was entrusted to them (cf. 1 Peter 3:15; Titus 1:9). With the Christian faith under constant attack from materialism, natural evolution, and secular and anti-Christian forces, evangelism has become not only a proclamation, but also a defense of the gospel against the other options offered to humans to satisfy their need for the divine and self-realization. Ministers use theological argumentation as they try to deconstruct the existential and conceptual paradigms of meaning offered by a secular or a non-Christian society, in order to show the meaningfulness, relevance, and the unique salvific power of the gospel of Jesus Christ. This is apologetics at its best. The Spirit can use this combination of theological thinking with evangelistic outreach to move the hearts of the listeners to repentance and conversion.

Apologetics are also important within the church itself as pastors seek to nurture their parishioners (2 Timothy 1:13, 14). Within Adventism, we confront attacks from former Adventists whose personal religious frustrations have led them to try to find ways to undermine the consistency and relevance of our end-time message. Pastors and theologians have the responsibility of protecting the flock from attacks that will undermine their faith and commitment to Jesus, His church, and the mission He entrusted to His people. The effectiveness of this defense of the faith depends on the ability of pastors to understand the theological issues involved, and on their capacity to couch the biblical and theological arguments in simple and effective language. With the nurturing of the congregation as important as doing public evangelism, we must do the former without neglecting the last.

4. Ministry and theology: Sermon preparation. Theologians share their findings mainly through teaching and writing, and ministers do it through the proclamation of the Word. Describing preaching as the ministerial activity through which the theological function of pastors becomes more visible can probably be classed as correct. Preaching presupposes that ministers spent time on their knees studying the Scriptures, reflecting on it, and dialoguing with the writings of theologians, while doing the exegetical work that will result in a solidly biblical sermon. As a result of that preparation, the pulpit becomes the place where the minister clearly proclaims the gospel, instructs the community of believers, strengthens their faith, and reaffirms their commitment to Jesus through the hearing of the Word, empowering them for service.

During their pastoral training, prospective ministers receive an introduction to the art of exegesis, to the tools needed for that task, and to the preparation of the sermon itself. As indicated above, they should not leave the seminary without those tools, but on the contrary, they should continue to use that knowledge, sharpening its use throughout their ministry. Pastors have the ethical responsibility of sharing with their parishioners biblically reliable and sound theological knowledge. Since every sermon should comprise biblically centered content, doing a proper exegesis is unavoidable. The exegetical task requires the use of Bible dictionaries and commentaries that could help in gaining a better understanding of the text.

Sermon preparation should motivate pastors to remain theologically well informed. One could even say that in the preparation of a sermon a dialogical bridge is created between pastors and theologians. However, for pastors, the final arbiter of meaning lies in the text itself. In this case, the pastor's personal knowledge of the Scriptures and of the message and mission of the church plays a fundamental role in the evaluation of theological discourses. *It should be clearly and unambiguously established that what pastors are to proclaim is not what theologians believe, but the message of the Scriptures* (2 Timothy 2:15). Therefore, they have to develop a deep understanding of the Word of God that will enable them to evaluate different theological perspectives in order to take to the pulpit and proclaim the biblical message and not human inventions, opinions, and theories. The authority of their proclamation does not depend on the renowned name of the theologian quoted in the sermon, but on the scriptural basis of their message.

Useful for pastors, as long as it is grounded in Scripture, theology seeks to build up the church through a full commitment to the message and mission of the church. The discriminating use of theological materials by pastors requires from them not only knowledge of the diversity of theological opinions in the church, but particularly a deep, personal comprehension and dedication to the message and mission of the church. All of this requires from pastors a significant development of their theological knowledge and a critical and discerning attitude towards the results of theological investigation.

5. *Ministers and theologians: Constant dialogue.* If we understand the theological role of pastors correctly, there has to be a constant dialogue between theologians and pastors. This suggests that theology is to a large extent a collective activity of the church as the body of Christ. The dialogue will contribute to remind theologians that they function as such not apart from the church, but as a needed component of it. As indicated already, their work should be motivated by the need to minister to the church and to the world at large. Pastors will benefit by the constant dialogue with theologians by being reminded that the message they proclaim stays rooted in the deep mysteries of God. They, like the theologians, have to dig deep in the Scriptures, in order to understand and be better prepared to proclaim the gospel in a meaningful and persuasive form to the church and to the world.

The recognition of the collective nature of theological development, and the need for pastors and theologians to be in constant dialogue, requires the direct involvement of church administrators in the dialogue. They should facilitate the communication through seminars, professional development courses for ministers, and by making accessible to pastors theological materials that will contribute to building the theology, message, and mission of the church. When church leaders put the emphasis on the evangelistic task at the exclusion of the theological development of pastors, the effectiveness of the overall nature of the ecclesiastical ministry becomes weakened with the nurturing of the church put at risk. However, when pastors put the emphasis on the theological task and the nurturing of church members at the almost total exclusion of the evangelistic work, they, in the long run, put at risk the very existence of their own congregations. Pastors and administrators should cooperate in shaping a well-rounded and properly equipped ministry to fulfill the gospel commission and should consider this of great importance.

Conclusion

Theology and pastoral ministry are not to be sundered; what God united, humans should not pull apart. The nature, role, and realization of the pastoral ministry are essentially determined by biblical theology. Ministry is an expression of God's intention for His church and, consequently, we identify it as of theological nature; we comprehend it better when we reflect on the God who lovingly provided this gift to His church and on the nature of that gift. Therefore, the question does not center on whether pastors should function as theologians, but whether or not they will effectively perform their pastoral/theological task or mission.

Pastors particularly deal with important theological issues when they interpret for their congregations the mission and message of the church. They experience direct involvement in the theological work when they stand for a message under attack, and when they prayerfully work on their sermons for their congregations. Interacting with theologians in the development of their theological knowledge should be considered important. However, the foundation of their theology and the content of their proclamation have to be firmly grounded on God's self-revelation in Scripture.

---

1. Walter Bauer, W. F. Arndt, F. W. Gingrich, and F. W. Danker, *A Greek-English Lexicon of the NT and Other Early Christian Literature,* 3rd ed. (Chicago, IL: University of Chicago Press, 2000), 449. For a study on the history of the term *theology,* consult F. Whaling, "The Development of the Word 'Theology,' " *Scottish Journal of Theology* 34 (1981): 289–312.

2. D. F. Wright, "Theology," in *New Dictionary of Theology,* ed. Sinclair B. Ferguson, David F. Wright, and J. I. Parker (Downers Grove, IL: InterVarsity Press, 1988), 680.

3. T. C. O'Brien, "Theologian," in *Encyclopedic Dictionary of Religion,* vol. 3, ed. Paul Kevin Meagher, Thomas C. O'Brien, and Consuelo Maria Aherne (Washington, DC: Corpus Publication, 1979), 3496. Cf. J. Daane, "Theology," in *International Standard Bible Encyclopedia,* vol. 4, ed. Geoffrey W. Bromiley (Grand Rapids, MI: Eerdmans, 1988), 827.

4. This type of theology has been called "personal theology," understood as "that which is done as the individual church member studies his or her Bible, attempting to relate it to the realities of everyday life. . . . It may easily become myopic, self-centered,

and limited in its ability to relate itself to others in the church or world at large." Willmore D. Eva, "Embracing the Role of Pastoral Theology," *Ministry,* October 1998, 4. Whenever theology is done in isolation from the community of believers, the dangers listed by Eva become real and threatening to the church.

5. One of the areas in which biblical theology should determine pastoral practices is the worship service. Biblical liturgy in the Old and New Testaments is theologically rich because at its very center is the person of God. Every worship act seeks to adore Him, to thank Him for His many blessings, and to ask for His company and blessings. Every innovation should be evaluated from that theological perspective, in order to determine whether it contributes to that end, distracts from it, or places the human beings at the center. Perhaps a specific example can be used to illustrate the importance of theological analysis before the pastor makes and implements certain decisions. When pastors decide that during the Communion service the Lord's Supper will be celebrated before footwashing, they are showing lack of theological perception. The order of the two ritual acts carry with it theological significance. Preserving that order is an act of submission to the will of the Savior who established the specific order. For Him, the Supper precedes the footwashing in the same way that covenant fellowship precedes God's redemptive act of salvation in Christ.

6. Wallace M. Alston Jr. has correctly stated that, "Christian theology without ministerial motivation simply does not exist and is found in the form of a pretender. The church, and particularly the congregation, is the locus of the ministry of Christian theology, and pastoral occasions test and evaluate its reality." "The Ministry of Christian Theology," in *Theology in the Service of the Church* (Grand Rapids, MI: Eerdmans, 2000), 19.

7. The idea that theology is, in a sense, faith, seeking understanding goes in principle back to Augustine. He wrote, "Dost thou wish to understand? Believe. . . . For understanding is the reward of faith. Therefore do not seek to understand in order to believe, but believe that thou mayest understand." *Tractatus in Joannis* 29.6, in *Nicene and Post-Nicene Fathers,* vol. 7, ed. Philip Schaff (Reprinted; Peabody, MA: Hendrickson, 2004), 184. The more common expression of the idea comes from Anselm: "For I do not seek to understand in order to believe but I believe in order to understand. For I believe even this: that I shall not understand unless I believe." *Proslogion* 1.

8. Eva perceptively comments concerning pastoral theology, "Here the attempt is made to relate the revelation of God in the Bible and in life to the ebbs and flows, highs and lows, joys and sorrows, of the people of the congregation. Because of its rough-and-tumble nature and the almost raw, organic constraints that are part and parcel of doing it, this theology unearths, when conducted with any care, some of the purest forms of truth. In many ways it is the kind of theology done by the characters and writers of the Bible itself." ("Embracing the Role," 4).

Chapter 3

The Pastor as a Visionary

R. Clifford Jones

Pastor Smith, as we shall call him, was having trouble falling asleep. His head swirled and his heart pounded as he tried to recount and process the events that had turned his church board meeting that evening into a vile, venomous verbal fight of accusations and recriminations. Slipping out from under the covers, he left his wife in bed (they had married while he was still in seminary) and tiptoed to his study, where he slumped into a chair. His hands cupping his chin, Smith began to muse about where and how things had gone wrong in his ministry.

Smith was not a bad pastor. He was used to giving adequate amounts of time to sermon preparation, and his sermons, almost always reflective of theological depth and clarity, were generally well received. Smith was organized and punctual in keeping appointments and getting back to people. Though not a youth pastor in the classic sense, he was appreciated by them, who found his genuineness refreshing. The older members especially liked that their pastor devoted a good portion of each week to visiting them in their homes. In short, Pastor Smith was approachable, available, and accessible.

Yet if one word were used to describe the overall mood at Smith's church that word would be *apathy*. Or perhaps *boredom*. After three years of ministering to this congregation, no one was sure in which direction Smith was taking it. When pressed to share his vision for the church,

Smith usually demurred, saying that he was waiting to hear from God. In time, the members simply stopped asking, and inertia and the doldrums set in.

The congregation's discontent with Smith's leadership exploded at the church board meeting that night when a request for a large disbursement of funds was made. Several board members protested the expenditure, claiming that it was directed toward maintenance ministry and symptomatic of the absence of a coherent, compelling vision of where the congregation was headed. These members were quick to stress that while they thought Smith was strong in the area of pastoral nurture, they thought he came up short in the area of leadership, especially when it came to vision-casting. Frustrated that the members felt that they lacked a clear sense of where the church was headed, that night members again pressed for answers, and Smith, caught off guard, stuttered through a few incoherent comments. As Smith slouched behind his desk in the darkness of his study with the ticking of the clock on the wall rhythmically breaking up the silence, he could not help but admit that what he had heard at the church board meeting that night was essentially correct.

The importance of vision

To drive a wedge between leadership and vision can be described as well-nigh impossible. Pick up any book on leadership and, almost always, it will have much to say about the fundamentally significant role vision plays in leadership. The leaders who succeed at influencing people are those who are able to forge and cast compelling visions. A visionless leader is an oxymoron. Such a person may succeed at management, but not leadership. When former president George Bush stated that he lost his bid to be re-elected president of the United States because of the vision thing, he was being insightful and penetrating. I am unaware of any leader who achieved greatness while lacking a vision around which people could coalesce and be empowered.

Vision separates the dreamers from the doers. Vision energizes, motivates, informs, shapes, creates a climate, sets a tone, raises the bar, triggers passion, and engenders action. Nothing of substance or worth has ever been accomplished but that a vision had first been cast. Leaders are doomed to irrelevance, if not failure, without vision. Some years ago, the American Express Company used as its advertising slogan, "The American Express Card: Don't Leave Home Without It." So central and crucial is vision to leadership that it might well be said, "Vision: Don't Leave Home Without It." A pastor bereft of vision can be likened to an armless person trying to pitch baseball. After a pastor's personal relationship with God, vision becomes the most important resource of a pastor.

Vision injects purpose and life into an organization. Almost always a unifying force, vision gives people common issues around which they may rally and to which they may offer their financial support. An operating principle in the field of philanthropy incorporates the concept that people do not support needs but visions. Fund-raisers know that parading the dire financial straits into which an organization has come will neither excite nor inspire potential donors as will sharing with them the vision of the organization.

Yet, according to George Barna, most pastors are clueless as to God's vision for their ministry, and even though most church members understand vision as a concept, many lack a strategic vision for their own lives. Barna notes that seminaries and educational institutions that exist to impart and enhance the tools of people for ministry do not generally use the vision statements of applicants to screen out people or place others in certain tracks. He also says that notwithstanding the vision statements of many churches, few have a program or provide opportunities intended to guarantee the realization of their vision. The bottom line is that vision, though trumpeted as a hallmark, if not the foundation of effective leadership, is more often spoken about than practiced effectively.[1]

Vision: What is it?

What is vision? As much as vision as a concept is in vogue these days, exactly what defines it seems confusing. Often spoken of as a synonym of mission, purpose, goal, or objective, vision can be defined as a mental image or picture of the future. Barna views it as "foresight with insight based on hindsight."[2] It is a "clear mental picture of a preferable future imparted by God to His chosen servants and is based upon an accurate understanding of God, self and circumstances."[3] When Robert Kennedy stated that some people, on seeing things as they are, asked "Why?" but he saw things that were not and asked instead "Why not?" he was conveying the essence of a vision.

Mission and vision go together but are not synonymous. A mission statement identifies an organization and captures, cogently and succinctly, what the group is all about. Objectives are the stuff of mission statements set forth in sublime and broad language. Other than for the element of identity, a mission statement may be applied to other churches—something that cannot be done with a vision statement. Vision statements are specific and unique even in terms of outcomes. For example, a mission statement may be, "The Faith Seventh-day Adventist Church exists to make disciples of all people, readying them for the second coming of Jesus Christ." A vision statement that goes along with this mission statement may be, "At the Faith Seventh-day Adventist Church, we envision a congregation of three hundred discipled Christians empowered by the Holy Spirit for service and impacting our community for Christ."

Mission can be described as parent to vision, the former dealing with the *why* of ministry, the reason the organization exists. Vision encapsulates the *what* of ministry, painting a picture of what the successful achievement of the mission of the organization will look like. A vision is the end product; it does not deal with things as they currently exist and eschews the *status quo*. That was the problem with Pastor Smith's ministry—it was focused on the present—just giving attention to current matters.

Elements of a good vision

Certain elements of Barna's definition of vision immediately grab our attention. Even though vision is future-focused, its anchor resides in the past and present. Vision does not ignore or discount past or present realities. On the contrary, vision takes inventory of them as it frames the future. Vision takes note of capacities and challenges, juxtaposing them against the promises and power of God, and vision focuses on results, on outcomes. It pictures what can be or will be as the result of the accomplishment of a mission. With God central to vision, He imparts the vision, and the visionary, whose understanding of or walk with God is impaired, stands to miss the vision.

For visions to be worth anything they must be sharp and clearly stated, for fuzzy, blurred visions confuse and do not motivate. A clear vision is a compelling vision, and you know you have a clear vision when others are able to picture and articulate it as well as you can. A compelling vision appeals to our better, nobler instincts, challenging us to stretch ourselves, to depart from our comfort zones, and to abandon the plains of mediocrity. Shades of sacrifice and strain are necessary components of a compelling vision, and though grounded in present realities, we are encouraged to scale heretofore unconquered territory. Although it stretches us, a vision is doable. Conceiving of and pursuing dreams hopelessly out of reach is ultimately frustrating, leading to low morale and leader burnout.

Admitting that visions take note of the present, even as they look to the future, does not say that visioning is by nature cautious or conservative. To be sure, a vision should be realistic, but also daring. Visionary leaders take risks, stretching themselves and resources to make the seemingly impossible possible. They hear things to which others are deaf, and they see things others do not. Visionary leaders believe that because the Almighty God, who can do anything but fail, gave them the vision, all things are possible. Consequently, they pursue their vision with optimism and a sense of accomplishment.

The Source of visions

God must ever be the Source of a pastor's vision. The pastor who fails to include God in the visioning process is destined to end up with a vision replete with selfish, mundane elements. The human heart, apart from the converting, regenerating action of God, remains powerless to cast aside its sinful inclinations to power and ambition and to place self before others. A vision that does not have God's imprint may rally a church to action and may even generate what appears to be kingdom success. Yet, in the long run, it will be seen for what it truly is—a temporary mirage bereft of lasting value.

In seeking to discover God's vision for themselves and their congregations, pastors will invest inordinate amounts of time in growing closer to God through Bible study, prayer, meditation, fasting, and journaling.[4] Establishing deadlines for the discovery or receipt of the vision should be resisted, for we never know just when God will act and how He will act. It behooves us to be open to God's leading and revelation, no matter how long that takes.

How will the pastor know for sure that a vision came from God? Visions from God lift up and glorify God, not the church, the pastor, or anything or anybody else. And because Christianity continues as more a relationship than a religion, God-breathed visions almost always focus on people, not programs or things.

Often, congregations want their pastors to do their visioning for them. I've heard of more than one congregation who posed to its newly installed pastor the question: "Pastor, what's your vision for this congregation?" Elaborating on this question, members are inclined to ask, "What do you think God is calling you to do in this place and at this time?" Though well-meaning, those who pose questions like these betray a gross misunderstanding of how a community of believers, called a church, comes to discover and embrace a vision of what God expects of that community. Moreover, pastors who outline a vision for a congregation at their first church board meeting, when chances are that the pastor knows very little about that new congregation, set themselves up for a rough ride. To be sure, all pastors should have a vision of their congregations being a community that reflects Christ's love as it witnesses to God's activity in the world. Yet we're not talking about that here—we are discussing context-specific vision.

Congregations that defer or relegate the visioning activity to their pastors may do so because they feel ill-equipped. They may think that only a person called by God has the qualifications to engage in the process, and may even believe that they do not have the time or energy to give to the process the deep level of engagement it deserves. Some cultures expect that a vision for a congregation should be handed down by a pastor, and some "higher" organizations do just that in collaboration with or through the pastor. Further, pastors who balk at revealing their vision may be viewed as not doing their job, as weak leaders not worth following, or worse, as lazy and lethargic.

While on occasions pastors may receive their visions in the solitariness of their study, more often than not visions emanate from a shared, mutual engagement of the community of faith. The days of "Lone Ranger" ministry have passed long ago, and the pastor who shows up at a board or business meeting claiming that after a season of private prayer God informed him or her to tell the congregation the direction in which it should go, may well be received with skepticism, if not animosity. At the very least, that pastor is guilty of a woeful lack of tact and professional courtesy.

Visions are embraced and pursued more readily when the congregation buys in, and this is most likely to happen if the congregation was a sought-after and appreciated participant in the visioning process from its beginning. The astute pastor will seek broad participation in the visioning process, fostering and cultivating vigorous engagement from all stakeholders.

Emphasizing that pastors should seek broad participation in the visioning process if a church's vision will be readily embraced by its congregants does not mean that the role of the pastor in the process has become secondary or inconsequential. On the contrary, the role of the pastor is crucial, and the ultimate responsibility for a church's vision rests on the pastor. Pastors must be key players in the visioning process, making sure that it begins, is fair and participated in by a representative cross-section of members, and culminates in a well-stated, easily grasped vision statement. Along the way, the pastor may have played the role of coach or active player, but never should it be said that he or she was a spectator.

Communicating the vision

Forming a vision is one thing, and how pastors communicate a vision becomes, in a sense, as important as the vision itself. As such, pastors need to be fully aware of the principles and dynamics of communication, paying particular attention to this in the context of leadership. Pastors will want to be sure that they do not communicate a vision in a holier-than-thou, condescending manner. Such an approach will almost certainly make for a less-than-robust acceptance of the vision. Pastors will also want to be sure to cast a vision broadly and to provide ample opportunity for dialogue and feedback so that, if necessary, tweaking or modifications of the vision may be done.

Dealing with resistance

To expect that a vision will receive 100 percent endorsement shows naivety. The adversary of the church will never allow a vision that has been formed and shaped by God to be warmly embraced by an entire congregation. The spirit of Sanballat et al. is anything but dead in the contemporary Christian church, a fact that should actually cause pastors to be leery if a wholehearted endorsement of a vision will ever happen.

Aubrey Malphurs identifies and expands on three categories of vision busters: vision vultures, vision vampires, and vision firemen. Vision vultures are nitpickers who dissect a vision piece by piece, while vision vampires explicate all the substance out of a vision. Vision firemen douse the vision with so much negative comment that its flames quickly burn out.[5] These three categories of people have in common a desire to torpedo the vision of the group for one reason or another. Their methods of resistance may be overt or covert, and may be short term or long term. Interestingly, many resisters have what they consider to be good, pure motives, believing firmly that they have the best interests of the entire church at heart, and many cloak their resistance in the garment of expertise and knowledge. Vision busters mouth comments such as, "We know what is best for this church," "We know what will work and not work here," and "We've been around a long time."

Why do well-meaning people oppose visions? The reasons run the gamut—cowardice, resistance to change, fear of the future, an unwillingness to invest resources, and a spirit of nonchalance and noninvolvement. Not surprisingly, sometimes people trigger opposition who are hurt because they were overlooked in the visioning process. Worse, some may resist the vision because they have a personal ax to grind.

A pastor responds to those in opposition to the church's vision depending on their tactics. If they are acting as snipers, surfacing only to lob shots at the vision and then quickly retreating for cover, they should be confronted or exposed. Snipers are usually cowards who, when confronted publicly, lose their power to intimidate. Vision vultures, vampires, and firemen should be sought out by the pastor, in preferably on a one-on-one setting, where the pastor will attempt to get at the reason for their opposition. Once pastors know the basis of the opposition, they should address it honestly, assuaging whatever misgivings the opponents may have. Should the opponent be a "key" church member, the proverbial E. F. Hutton in the congregation, the pastor will not discount the importance of getting this individual on board. Still, pastors should not compromise their integrity or values to win anybody over believing that a God-given vision will succeed in spite of resistance from the most powerful or most influential church member.

Summary

The pastor who cannot be categorized as a visionary most likely will not be an effective leader. After their relationship with God, vision becomes the most valuable resource a Christian pastor can have. It behooves pastors, therefore, to spend time discovering and clarifying God's vision for their ministry, and to invest energy in partnering with their congregations in knowing and pursuing God's vision for their parish.

---

1. George Barna, *The Power of Vision* (Ventura, CA: Regal Books, 2003), 9, 10.

2. Ibid., 24.

3. Ibid.

4. Ibid., 78–82.

5. Aubrey Malphurs, *Developing a Vision for Ministry in the 21st Century* (Grand Rapids, MI: Baker Book House, 1999), 177, 178.

Chapter 4

The Pastor and the Local Church

Benjamin D. Schoun

In the past, it was assumed that ministry was done in and through a local congregation. Where else? This can no longer be an automatic assumption. More and more pastors[1] that I know do not serve congregations but rather work in counseling ministries, chaplaincy, consultancy, denominational ministries, independent evangelistic, music, or media ministries, and any number of other parachurch or independent ministries.[2] Often these parachurch ministries are prominent, thriving, and well funded in contrast to the often discouraging challenges of local church life. Furthermore, contemporary trends reflect that many people in society are attracted to spirituality but not interested in a connection to the organized church. Just how important, then, is the church for Christian ministry? In this chapter, we will first reflect on the relationship between ministry and the local church, and then address several important facets of the pastor's work in the context of a local congregation.

The local church's centrality for ministry

The relationship between congregational and parachurch ministries raises the question of how one should define *church*. Without getting into the complex details of ecclesiology, we can say that while other types of ministries may be part of the church, the local congregation is the most basic understanding of church as the Scriptures describe it. Jesus founded the church, described it as His body, and invested in no other organization the same promise of His presence and spiritual authority. Other organizations may have very focused ministries, but the church carries the broad responsibility of the gospel commission. The local congregations conduct baptisms and hold church membership. It is the place of weekly worship and the storehouse for tithes and offerings, the place where people come together in community, and where God works through the body in unity and authority to protect the true faith in accordance with the Scriptures. The church represents God's people in the broadest sense, and stands as the hub to which all other activities and ministries should relate.

A pastor's work, including every supporting ministry, should not be done in isolation; it must be integrally tied to the church, with the church as the center. The pastor and other ministries are servants to the church. This is not to say that parachurch ministries should not exist. It *is* to say that parachurch ministries need to take responsibility for creating intentional linkages to the church. It *is* to say that laity needs to support, with time, talent, and financial gifts, the work of the church so that it, too, will have vibrant, exciting ministries. It *is* to say that pastors need to make use of the best professional tools and processes to move the church into an active, attractive, Spirit-filled church life. With a lot of room for the local church to be all it can be as the central site for ministry, members may still need to change forms or style so that it can become the most successful, attractive, appealing place to be.

Such a vision of the local church requires new thinking on the part of the denomination and its leaders, as well as a new focus among the members. But there are also things that the pastor can do to help create this new reality. In fact, the role of the pastor is essential, with this principle widely recognized in church-growth literature. William M. Easum says, "The single most important factor in determining the growth of a church is the pastor's attitude about its mission."[3] Because of this, Easum also suggests that longer tenures increase the likelihood for growth to occur. Commenting on the trends of the world's largest churches, John Vaughan says, "The pastor is unquestionably a key to the growth of the churches."[4] In the "natural church development" program created by Christian Schwarz, the first quality characteristic of a healthy church is "empowering leadership."[5] If this is true, what are the most important things that a pastor can do to help make the church a thriving center of ministry?

The pastor's central role in local church ministry

Not many definitions in Scripture of the work of the pastor can be found. The word *pastor* refers to shepherding of the flock. However, we must be careful not to read into this biblical usage a priority on what we know today as psychologically based counseling ministries. Rather, it should be understood in a much more comprehensive sense of moving the church and its members forward in a life of health and purpose. One of the spiritual gifts enumerated in the New Testament includes the office of pastor. Ephesians 4, however, is the only passage that specifically mentions the pastoral gift. The chapter begins with a reference to the "calling" of all of God's people (verse 1), and to the fact that every follower of Christ has been given a "grace" or a "gift" (verse 7). But *some* were given the gift of being apostles, prophets, evangelists, pastors, and teachers (verse 11). This cluster of gifts has a particular purpose or job— "for the equipping of the saints for the work of ministry" (verse 12, NKJV). We can call these the leadership gifts because they prepare the larger membership for various other kinds of ministries.[6] This should be recognized as a monumentally significant concept, for too many times the pastor personally does a majority of the acts of ministry rather than involving the larger number of congregational members. But this defining text clearly points out that the central role of a pastor is to equip other members for service!

Research has demonstrated that this is one of the strongest determining factors affecting church health and growth. George Barna states, "Intentional outreach will fail to have a significant impact, though, unless the ministry is undertaken by the congregation rather than just by the paid professionals. Keeping this in mind, turnaround pastors gave top priority to *equipping the laity for effective, targeted ministry.* Indeed, until the people believed enough in themselves as ministers on God's behalf, there was little chance that they would believe the church could sustain a comeback."[7]

Many of the other roles of a pastor, even those included in this book, can be done by lay members. Lay members can preach, lead worship, counsel, evangelize, give Bible studies, and chair boards and committees. But because of the pastor's call to leadership, because of their gift for the function of ministry (in most cases they receive special training for it and do the work of ministry full time), that person is in a unique position to lead and teach others how to do ministry. A pastor cannot *do* all the ministry that needs to be done. No doubt, there are some aspects of ministry that the pastor will do, but the emphasis should be on involving the entire force of workers in the congregation.

Ellen White says it quite plainly, " 'The best help that ministers can give the members of our churches is . . . planning work for them.' "[8] "Let the minister devote more of his time to educating than to preaching. Let him teach the people how to give to others the knowledge they have received."[9]

Church growth guru Robert Logan likes to envision the role of a pastor as similar to a coach of a sports team. "Just as a coach equips his or her team to win, so an effective pastor functions like a coach to cultivate a thriving congregation."[10] Attempts have been made in various parts of the Seventh-day Adventist denomination to encourage this model as a new paradigm for ministry.[11]

Space does not permit a detailed elaboration of the equipping roles and their applications, but the most important elements involve leadership, teaching or coaching, and managing. Leadership largely has to do with the casting of a vision; this vision, then, reflects and details the mission of the organization. Vision-casting does not necessarily tell people what they must do, but portrays an outcome in a way that attracts, inspires, and motivates. Leadership results in pulling people together in collaborative, prayerful planning. Using professional skills that the pastor has developed, the group moves toward building consensus. The leader guides the process through diverse viewpoints and conflicts as they outline clear, doable strategic plans.

Teaching or coaching gives members the knowledge and skills they need, building upon their spiritual gifts to do an outstanding job in fulfilling the plans. Managing includes the tasks of providing resources, structure, monitoring, troubleshooting, and rewards for the workers. Some of these managing tasks can be delegated to subordinate leaders, but a pastor finds it difficult to avoid the leading and coaching roles.

The pastor's need for adaptability to the local congregation

Another key element for the success of pastors in relationship to congregations can be identified as adaptability. Pastors should recognize the importance of having a strong sense of the ideal, a clear goal for the future, and a long-term plan for achieving it. But in the near term, local churches differ and success requires "different strokes for different folks."

Some years ago, Arlin J. Rothauge wrote an analysis of churches of four different sizes and how that one factor affected the way each church carried out its ministry, how it attracted new members, and the implications for leadership in each setting.[12] This classification has since become an important reference point for other studies in congregational life.[13] Rothauge labeled the four categories: Family Church (up to 50 members), Pastoral Church (50–150 members), Program Church (150–350 members), and the Corporation Church (350–500 members and over). In the Family Church, the pastor will function as a chaplain and the head of the family (church) is a local matriarchal or patriarchal member. The next category, as the name suggests, centers around the pastor. Almost everything revolves around the pastor and if pastors are wise, they will find others to share in the leadership. In the Program Church, the laity becomes even more important since the pastor can no longer maintain close contact with everyone in the congregation. The roles of leading, equipping, and managing become essential. The central pastoral role in the Corporation Church can be described as more symbolic and legendary. Here the leadership role of vision-casting is most important, whereas the operation of the church moves forward with a complexity of staff members, boards, secondary leaders, groups, and volunteers. This brief overview suggests the adaptability that a pastor must have in various situations.

Leadership styles must vary according to the situation and personality of a church. Some congregations may not have a wide variety of gifts represented in their membership because of small size or other circumstances. In some cases, pastors may need to *do* certain roles that might otherwise be best shared with members. The goal includes what is necessary to make the church healthy, but not to do what members can and should be doing. Pastors will always be seeking to work themselves out of a job here or there as persons emerge who can take up that ministry.

The pastor's authority in the local church

One of the most ambiguous aspects of the relationship between a pastor and the local church lies in the issue of authority. Sometimes both the pastor and members do not know for sure how this works. Some pastors assert themselves as the final word. In other situations, committees or congregations do the same and they delight in keeping pastors in their place. Other churches willingly submit or even seek clear, decisive directions from the pastor. How much authority does a pastor really have?

In the Seventh-day Adventist Church, the place of greatest authority happens in the most widely represented church meetings. In the local church, this occurs in a church business meeting. At the General Conference level, it is at the world session held every five years. Because these bodies do not meet very often, in between these meetings boards or executive committees hold the most authority. From the perspective of organizational structure, a pastor cannot veto an action of the church board, nor can a conference president overrule a conference committee, but a conference committee can overrule a president. These leaders have delegated authority; they have the power of influence, the authority of respect, and a prophetic voice. They do not have independent decision-making authority unless given to them by the governing body. Some boards and committees allow a leader to exercise autocratic authority, but they need not do so according to Adventist organizational structure.

The pastors will be the most successful when they find that balance between clear, consistent, inspiring, visionary leadership, while not over-assuming power in an autocratic manner. A pastor does have a great deal of influence, but not a great amount of decision-making power. Actually, it is better this way because it encourages participatory processes that instill ownership, motivation, and participation among the members.

The pastor's relationships with members

One other area that can have a significant effect on ministry in the local church and continues as a source of uncertainty in a pastor's life lies in how they should relate personally to the members of the congregation. If the pastor develops certain close friendships, other members may feel slighted and accuse them of having favorites. Some members have such high expectations for the pastoral family, with no allowance for them to live as normal human beings, and this has been sometimes referred to as a pastoral pedestal. Others may see the pastor on that pedestal as aloof, artificial, hiding behind a mask, or without authenticity. Worse still, the pastor may, in fact, be actually living in that unreal world. But if pastor jumps off the pedestal to become a fellow human being, he or she may land in a pool of alligators that could quickly tear him or her apart.

Because the best approach will be different from one congregation to another, pastors should always seek to be genuine and authentic, but without a need to reveal every personal thing about their private lives. Ministry is usually more effective if done as a "wounded healer," to use an image from Henri Nouwen[14]—that is, individuals who must bind up their own wounds, while also ministering to the wounds of others. Even when they are down-to-earth with other humans, pastors need to maintain a certain dignity for the office they represent. Always keep in mind that both pastors and members live on the same level as human beings before God. Their status remains the same; both are the people of God (laity). Only their roles may differ in terms of what God calls them to do.

While not considered wrong to have friendships among members, the pastor in the professional role should minister to people equitably. Do not favor personal friends in the context of professional capacities, and keep the boundaries between personal and professional relationships distinct. Church elders are the professional colleagues of pastors, and biblically they have the same leadership responsibilities. So developing friendships with elders can be considered appropriate and even advisable.

One safeguard in developing relationships with members includes making sure that self-disclosure proceeds from both sides on an equal basis. Don't reveal more than what the members are willing to reveal about themselves. As a pastor, make sure you have a mutual relationship. This will help protect the pastor from antagonists who may attack at a later time. I like the illustration of the way turtles explore their world, including other turtles. One turtle will stick his head out from under his shell just a little. If the other turtle reciprocates, the first turtle will venture a little further. Each one becomes a little more free as the other one makes itself more vulnerable in the same way. In this manner, trust is developed and eventually, increment by increment, their necks are both fully out in the sunlight, interacting in whatever way turtles do.[15]

Conclusion—know the end from the beginning

As Adventist Christians, we live in a world where we see growing evidences that supernatural forces are struggling for people's lives and allegiances. With every kind of diversion, philosophy, and temptation thrust in front of them to confuse and blind them to the message of God for their lives, it isn't easy to carry out the work God has given us to do. The church, often ignored, embattled, underfunded, and unattractive, has still been described as "God's appointed agency for the salvation of men."[16] Although discouraged at times, pastors are God's chosen leaders to help the church fulfill its mission. But the Word of God records a clear message about the requirements. "So then, men ought to regard us as servants of Christ and as those entrusted with the secret things of God. Now it is required that those who have been given a trust must prove faithful" (1 Corinthians 4:1, 2, NIV). That's our responsibility—to be faithful.

But there's more. We do know the outcome. God's church will accomplish its purpose. At the place of the very first mention of the word *church* in the New Testament, Christ already promised that the church would be built and the forces of evil would not overcome it (Matthew 16:17–19, NIV). He also said He has given the keys of the kingdom to the church. How reassuring to know the end from the beginning! The church will complete its task of ministry under God's direction with a positive and certain outcome. And all along the way, Christ promises to be with us. As He finishes His statement of the gospel commission, He finally says, " 'And surely I am with you always, to the very end of the age' " (Matthew 28:20, NIV). The church will be the center of ministry and faithful pastors will lead the church to its divine purpose using wise principles under the leadership of Jesus Christ and the power of the Holy Spirit.

---

1. Some may make a distinction between the word *pastor* and the word *minister,* the former being attached to a local congregation and the latter a religious worker who serves in any of a broader variety of ministries.

2. Jeffrey K. Haddon says, "The defining characteristic of a parachurch is that it stands outside of the organizational structure of well-established religious bodies" (in *Parachurch Organizations,* http://etext.lib.virginia.edu/relbroal/parachurch.htm, July 8, 1999).

3. William M. Easum, *The Church Growth Handbook* (Nashville: Abingdon Press, 1990), 56–58.

4. John N. Vaughan, "Trends Among the World's Twenty Largest Churches," in *Church Growth: State of the Art,* ed. C. Peter Wagner (Wheaton, IL: Tyndale House Publishers, 1986), 131.

5. Christian A. Schwarz, *Natural Church Development* (Carol Stream, IL: Church Smart Resources, 1996), 22.

6. The KJV places a comma in the first phrase of verse 12, suggesting that those people with the gifts that are mentioned, both equip the saints and do the work of ministry, whereas the better reading is that the leaders equip the saints so that the saints will do the work of ministry.

7. George Barna, *Turn-Around Churches: How to Overcome Barriers to Growth and Bring New Life to an Established Church* (Ventura, CA: Regal Books, 1993), 49.

8. Ellen G. White, *Testimonies for the Church* (Nampa, ID: Pacific Press® Publishing Association, 1948), 9:82.

9. White, *Testimonies for the Church,* 7:20.

10. Robert E. Logan, *Beyond Church Growth* (Grand Rapids, MI: Fleming H. Revell, 1989, 1995), 41.

11. Russell Burrill has been the strongest voice in this initiative through the SEEDS conferences that he has organized, and through his books, two of which address this

topic in some detail, *Revolution in the Church* (Fallbrook, CA: Hart Research Center, 1993), 48ff; and *Recovering an Adventist Approach to the Life and Mission of the Local Church* (Fallbrook, CA: Hart Research Center, 1998).

12. Arlin J. Rothauge, *Sizing up a Congregation for New Member Ministry* (New York: The Episcopal Church Center, n.d.).

13. Roy M. Oswald, "How to Minister Effectively in Family, Pastoral, Program, and Corporate Sized Churches," *Action Information* (Washington, DC: The Alban Institute), vol. XVII, no. 2, March/April 1991, 1–7, and vol. XVII, no. 3, May/June 1991, 5–7. (See also http://www.congregationalresources.org/article0132.asp.)

14. Henri J. M. Nouwen, *The Wounded Healer: Ministry in Contemporary Society* (Garden City, NY: Image Books, 1972, 1979).

15. Every pastor should have a well-designed support system. There is another chapter in this book on that subject.

16. White, *The Acts of the Apostles,* 9.

Chapter 5

The Pastor Relating to the Denomination

Alvin M. Kibble

Carl George, a sociologist and consultant for denominations across America, has worked for many years with the Seventh-day Adventist Church. In the early 1990s, George reportedly said that he wasn't sure whether Seventh-day Adventism was a church masquerading as an educational system, or an educational system masquerading as a church. His comments reflect the church's ownership and operation of one of the largest health corporations in America and the largest Protestant educational system. In addition, the church operates six insurance companies, manufactures health food, and has a conglomerate of publishing houses.

Yet with all of that, if we were to reduce the Seventh-day Adventist Church to its least common denominator, it would consist of a pastor and a local congregation. Amid the merits of ministry, institutions, and businesses owned and operated by the church, primary to its mission and authenticity resides the pastor and their flock. Before the emergence of the General Conference or even state conferences, there were pastors and churches.

The pastor may sense a special summons from God and in response prepare for ministry by enrolling in college and the seminary, but the conference must affirm that call by extending an invitation for church employment and assigning the pastor to a local congregation or district. In a practical sense, it may organizationally be said, "Many are called, but few are chosen."

Often used interchangeably, the terms *pastor* and *minister* refer to individuals who have the primary responsibility of caring for a flock, i.e., a local congregation of members.

A call for faithfulness

The pastor has been given the highest of callings. In the words of Brooklyn, New York's, pastor emeritus of the Concord Baptist Church of Christ, Dr. Gardner Taylor, he works for God & Son. A faithful performance of the duties assigned to the pastor should drive every one both into the vineyard and into their prayer chamber in earnest intercession with their Lord and Sponsor. The reason? Our congregations, our society, and the times we live in all demand far more from us. The congregation is a service organization with clients—both "the called out" and "those for whom we are sent." This is no time and this is no place for pastors who merely put in their time, going through the motions, giving only halfhearted effort. Today's ministry requires our strongest possible commitment that empowers, drawing forth our greatest potential and making us valued team members.

The apostle Paul felt the importance of such faithfulness testifying of his own ministry in Christ, "We proclaim him, admonishing and teaching everyone with all wisdom, so that we may present everyone perfect in Christ. To this end I labor, struggling with all his energy, which so powerfully works in me" (Colossians 1:28, 29, NIV). As Seventh-day Adventist pastors, we are responsible to God, to our supervising conference, and to ourselves to prepare our flock for Christ's return. We advance God's work through humble but bold leadership, through respect for our brethren at both the congregation and conference levels, and through the pastor's personal commitment to continual spiritual growth and professional development. "It is God who works through His pastors both to will and then to do of His good pleasure." If such becomes their personal regimen, realized in all its fullness, the pastor can prayerfully minister to the spiritual growth and development of the entirety of their congregation.

Pastoral office

Jesus instructed His disciples, " 'The kings of the Gentiles lord it over them; and those who exercise authority over them call themselves Benefactors. But you are not to be like that. Instead, the greatest among you should be like the youngest, and the one who rules like the one who serves' " (Luke 22:25, 26, NIV). As pastor of the local church, the minister again serves as the first servant of that church and not a lord to rule over it with force. They are the designated leaders of the church—commissioned by God and assigned by the employing conference. Paul counseled the early believers, "No one takes this honor upon himself; he must be called by God, just as Aaron was" (Hebrews 5:4, NIV).

As leader, the pastor must master a wide range of skills, from implementing and administrating processes to inspiring the membership in spiritual formation, growing in faith, in knowledge, in stewardship, and in discipleship. The pastor fills a number of roles, using a wide range of skills and leadership styles according to the task, the situation, and people involved. As a shepherd, the pastor leads, guides, and guards the flock of God. As a teacher, the pastor teaches and trains the people in the will and ways of God. As an apostle sent forth to advance the work of God, the pastor also is a preacher and an evangelist commissioned to share the everlasting gospel with those who live in darkness and who have no knowledge of God or of His Son, Jesus Christ.

If we are to understand the gospel commission in its most practical application, we would say that it includes making disciples for Christ—to prepare a people for the eminent return of our Lord. Accordingly, this work must be carried out in the marketplace—the community—by the frontline workers, pastors, and their congregations. At this level of the church, witness takes place with Bible studies given, sermons preached, individuals led to decision, and new believers brought into fellowship with the Lord and the body of Christ through the rite of baptism. So what is the relationship of the pastor to the conference? The pastor, in a spiritual sense, can be called the resident agent of the church at large and of the local conference. Employed and ordained by a conference, pastors have as their assignment being a minister of Christ, of the gospel, and of the church.

Whatever the church tries to say to the world, the pastor is its voice. Once ordained, the pastors or ministers live no longer on their own; they are stewards of Christ, of the mysteries of the gospel, and of the church.

As pastors, we must consider how we personally can increase our value to the church, better serve the members, build stronger community relationships, empower the laity, improve communications, increase trust, and advance the kingdom of grace. As essential pieces in the chain let down from heaven, we become a part of the great whole, and even though we are all in the mission together, every pastor's role becomes exclusively their own. Each of us must hold ourselves accountable for outcomes.

Fellow stewards and lifelong learners

Peter F. Drucker, the guru of American management, notes that knowledge is becoming the most important product. We must keep up with evolving events. As I heard an investment advertisement state, "You think you understand the situation, but what you don't understand is that the situation just changed."

As clergy, we are more than bean counters; we are capable of multiplying fish and loaves. However, we must be "wiser than those in Thessalonica," who were slow to learn and slow to change. Just as Paul's followers, we must be avid students of the Word and of the times, disposed to hear the gospel, void of bigotry and prejudice, and circumspect in our regard for one another. We must become lifelong students of the gospel if we are to share God's Word with our members. We can set no better model for those we pastor than this. As students, we will learn how to use our talents most wisely—our "spiritual, mental, and physical ability, the influence, station, possessions, affections, sympathies, all are precious talents to be used in the cause of the Master for the salvation of souls for whom Christ died."[1]

We must live as owners of our talents, not just workers. Each pastor must assume more personal responsibility for the success and completion of God's work. To function as an owner, a pastor must use peripheral vision, developing the ability to grasp the large picture while gaining a sense of the whole.

The role of the local conference

Here pastors' peripheral vision must tally with the overall vision cast abroad in their field by the employing organization: the local conference. In its field of operations, the local conference leadership provides its pastors, its staff workers, its teachers, and all of its other employees with a broad vision of the work to be accomplished for Jesus Christ, with experienced leadership, with strategic momentum, and with helpful guidance. Likened unto the New Testament work of bishops, pastors, too, are servants, for the Bible teaches that "the greatest among you will be your servant" (Matthew 23:11, NIV). "Serving as overseers—not because you must, but because you are willing . . . not lording it over those entrusted to you, but being examples to the flock" (1 Peter 5:2, 3, NIV).

An interesting term borrowed from the German business culture refers to "first among equals." One might say that, as conference leaders, they are within the organizational structure of the church, "first among equals." As employees and servants of the church, the pastor and other workers are accountable to the conference. Leaders, pastors, and all other employees share alike the trust relationship that together they have established with the Lord.

Based on the principle of the strong helping the weak, the conference provides a means of sharing the wealth of the family churches and socializing some of the operating costs and expenses of ministry. Following the global view of the church's mission—"the gospel to all the world"—the church has corporately established itself as an institution and entered into shared ministries and ventures for the advancement of its work. The sharing of tithe and distribution of freewill offerings is the preferred means of supporting the gospel ministry, especially in places where, without this support, the work would be seriously undermined or may not even exist. Every contribution counts! Church members should be valued partners who make a difference. Ministers need to add enough value to their mission so that their congregants see that something very important will be missing without them as a part of that mission.

As the employing organization, the conference provides in-service training for its pastors and ministerial staff. Categorized as high priority, these appointments should be carefully guarded and valued by each pastor. As a type of marathon career, ministry provides opportunities for retreats, in-services, workshops, and continuing education classes that are too rare to be neglected. The spin-off of collegiums of pastors and leaders in study adds another benefit as an essential team booster.

While the conference-scheduled workers' meetings or pastors' meetings cannot be considered an option, some pastors fail to recognize the importance of these appointments and allow petty distractions and un-monitored calendar conflicts to affect their attendance. As a result, the morale of fellow pastors has been negatively influenced, team-building efforts flawed, and the shared vision for mission compromised. We must guard conference appointments carefully.

How local conferences began

The early Adventist Church was charged with a responsibility to announce to the world the soon return of Jesus Christ. Then, as the three angels' messages (after 1844) were being preached and taught from town to town and from city to city, congregations began sprouting up to the point that it became necessary to organize them in order to advance the mission. One of the early leaders, John N. Loughborough, appealed to the delegates at a special conference in Battle Creek, during April 26–29, 1861, that the churches needed to organize in order to assure order in the church. In response, the delegates voted that a committee of nine ministers should develop a paper on church organization and publish it in *The Advent Review and Sabbath Herald*. The document, published on June 11, 1861, presented three important recommendations: (1) that future meetings of the General Conference should ensure representation from the various localities and congregations making up the Seventh-day Adventist movement; (2) that state or district conferences should be formed for the purpose of certifying those ministers representing the church, i.e., to eliminate imposters, as well as to ensure the supplying of churches in every part of the field with the means of coming together in their several states or districts for social and public worship and for the building up of each other in the Word of the Lord; and (3) that a more thorough organization of local churches be established for effective service and spiritual growth. More specifically, the memorial suggested that each church keep an up-to-date list of its members, that a letter-of-transfer system be developed for members in good standing who moved from one congregation to another, and that written records be kept of both business transactions and disciplinary cases.[2]

These organizations, referred to as state conferences, were intended to be supporting entities that insured administrative symmetry, doctrinal purity, and ministerial certification, while providing servant leadership and a much needed worldview.

Not sure if they even wanted to be called a denomination, the architects of these state conferences labored to incorporate into their structure the simplicity and form evidenced in the New Testament church. The General Conference assumed the general supervision of all of its branches, including the state conferences, and the state conferences provided supervision for all of its branches within the state, including the churches in that state.

Today's ministers should note, organizations and structures notwithstanding, that pastors and local congregations are still primary. In the evolution of things, individuals tended to overlook the principle building blocks of their society or organizations. Priorities shift and that which was once central becomes secondary. Organizations, like great sailing vessels, if not carefully monitored can drift off course. In this regard, we must all be mindful that the church exists for the congregations and not the congregations for the church. In other words, Christ gives the commission to individuals and the individuals, by partnering together, form ministries and churches. The organization resulted from their initiative to carry out the commission of Christ. Mission takes place in the marketplace, not in the corporate office.

Pastoral tenure

The pastoral tenure at an assigned church or district may vary from one conference to another. In earlier years within the Seventh-day Adventist

Church, tenure was usually brief, one to three years, maybe four. The reason was twofold: (1) there were only a few pastors employed by the church that, if you will recall, had as its mission field the entire world; and (2) there were limited talents even among those actively employed. Ellen White admonished,

> The question is asked me if it is not a mistake to remove the president of a State conference to a new field when many of the people under his present charge are unwilling to give him up.
>
> The Lord has been pleased to give me light on this question. I have been shown that ministers should not be retained in the same district year after year, nor should the same man long preside over a conference. A change of gifts is for the good of our conferences and churches.
>
> Ministers have sometimes felt unwilling to change their field of labor; but if they understood all the reasons for making changes they would not draw back.[3]

In the parable of the talents, each individual receives something from the Master, " 'To one he gave five talents of money, to another two talents, and to another one talent, each according to his ability. Then he went on his journey' " (Matthew 25:15, NIV). The master did not give to each man in the same measure. Paul reemphasized this in his letter to the believers at Ephesus, "It was he who gave some to be apostles, some to be prophets, and some to be evangelists, and some to be pastors and teachers, to prepare God's people for works of service, so that the body of Christ may be built up" (Ephesians 4:11, 12, NIV). Few of us have so many gifts that we can ensure a full offering of the pastoral skills needed to grow and to develop a church. We have our strengths; we also have our weaknesses. As children take on the mannerisms of their parents, so members their pastors. Through a wise plan of tenure and succession, the congregation can experience greater breadth, a more balanced spiritual and organizational development. The counsel that we were given here was that "some ministers need to move on before their character defects cause people to lose confidence."[4] Short-stay tenure was deemed a wiser and safer plan.

While engaged in ministry and under the pressure of everyday challenges, ministers can become so absorbed in their work that they have neither time nor opportunity to think and to reflect. Time for spiritual formation can become a luxury that few pastors feel they can afford. And under the sheer weight of it all, human nature takes over and pastors do what on the surface makes sense—they rely on what they do best. But what if conditions call for something entirely different? What if doing what we do best isn't working very well? When pastors do the wrong thing for their congregation, even if they do it well, the church's description reads trouble. The same qualities that may be considered a leader's strengths may become weaknesses when circumstances change but behavior doesn't. But with the completion of an assignment, time exists for reflection, renewal, careful assessment, and for professional improvement and growth. Both stimulating and rewarding, these timely reassignments may even provide what the academic culture refers to as a sabbatical.

Although we all must keep evolving, some pastors become despondent because they have to change. One conference president, when asked by a pastor why he was being moved, responded with a smile, "Well, you have made enough mistakes here; it's time to move on and get a fresh start!" With the increase in talent, expertise, and training, coupled with the complexity of ministry and rising costs of relocating, the length of tenure in our time has greatly increased. With few exceptions, young pastors, even interns, serve districts for five to seven years, senior pastors from seven to twelve years, and in a few instances, longer still. Yet the principle is still valid. Change is good for our conferences, good for our churches, and good for pastors.

A personal commitment to cooperation

Churches and conferences need a statement of purpose and core operating values. They greatly benefit from establishing guidelines and procedures for conflict resolution because all too often pastors involve themselves in casting blame. This method never strengthens character; to the contrary, it injures and weakens character. Conferences, for their part, too often operate as though pastors individually do not matter. We all must rise above such things. It has been said that "running an organization is easy when you don't know how, but very difficult when you do."

While generally assumed that local conference leadership holds accountability for morale, when either pastors or conference leaders make someone else entirely responsible for our morale, we weaken our own influence. Without a doubt, leadership sets the tone and the atmosphere of the organization, whether in a conference or in a church. If a church seems cold or unfriendly, one need look no further than its leader. Whether the conference or the church can be categorized as personal or impersonal, whether it fosters team building or one-on-one competition, or whether it controls or empowers, this has much to do with the person at the helm.

But as Christian leaders, we must have what Stephen R. Covey calls, "Response-ability"—the ability to respond appropriately in a given situation. We must act rather than react; we must determine to control our own attitudes and bring our sunshine with us. Complaining about a problem is not nearly as productive as contributing to its solution. Sitting around in casual moments, grousing over problems, believed or imagined, never helps. What is helpful is brainstorming collectively on possible solutions.

All spiritual leaders are open to criticism, and all too often we err. Unfortunately, our personnel files and historical documents reveal cases of the abuse of power by leaders, the disrespect by leaders of workers, and inequitable and unfair treatment. Preferential treatment, jealousy, and greed, as well as wage and hiring issues, have existed from the time of Christ. In some instances, Ellen White notes, "Shepherds [pastors] have been treated with reckless disregard by those in high positions."[5]

All of this and all who participate in such have been sufficiently rebuked by Ellen G. White. She advises,

> Not only have the sheep and lambs been dealt with in hardness,
> but even the shepherds themselves have been treated with reck-

less disregard. They have been spoken of in a way that shows that many in high and lower positions have little courtesy to give to God's ordained ministers. The churches themselves have been educated in such a way that they have had too little respect for those who preach the word of God, and who for years have given full proof of their ministry. But this way of dealing with the ministers and with the members of the family of God must be changed. The blessing of God cannot rest upon those who manifest little respect for the workers together with him.[6]

Workers together with God

Pastors should not act independently of the conference leadership. As well, though we have our specialized assignments and our individual responsibility before God, we should not, in our congregations, follow our own independent judgment disregarding the opinions and feelings of our congregants; this course leads to disorder in the congregation. The duty of pastors includes respecting the informed judgment of their members. In all things, their relations to one another, as well as the doctrines they teach, should be brought to the test of the law and testimony. With teachable hearts, there will be no division among us. Ellen White counsels that though "some are inclined to be disorderly, and are drifting away from the great landmarks of the faith . . . *God is moving upon His ministers to be one in doctrine and in spirit.*"[7]

Ownership: A valued partnership

In summary, the pastor and the local conference share a close and important partnership, each carrying different but necessary aspects of responsibility. In order to ensure the desired "vision to mission" objectives of the family of churches or conference, the pastor must share in the larger interest, support of, and concern for the organization. The solvency of the conference becomes an added value to the support of the local congregation, and this every pastor must understand and teach. As pastors, we rightly must display our *ownership* of all things done in Christ's name and Christ's cause.

1. Ellen G. White, "The Use of Talents," *The Advent Review and Sabbath Herald,* October 26, 1911, 3.

2. J. H. Waggoner, James White, J. N. Loughborough, E. W. Shortridge, Joseph Bates, J. B. Frisbie, M. E. Cornell, Moses Hull, and John Byington, "Conference Address: Organization," *The Advent Review and Sabbath Herald,* June 11, 1861, 21, 22.

3. Ellen G. White, *Manuscript Releases,* vol. 9 (Silver Spring, MD: Ellen G. White Estate, 1990), 143.

4. Ellen G. White, *Pastoral Ministry* (Silver Spring, MD: General Conference Ministerial Association, 1995), 102.

5. Ibid., 103.

6. Ellen G. White, "Brotherly Love Needed," *The Advent Review and Sabbath Herald,* October 24, 1893, 2.

7. Ellen G. White, *Testimonies to Ministers and Gospel Workers* (Mountain View, CA: Pacific Press® Publishing Association, 1962), 503; italics supplied.

Chapter 6

The Pastor as Worship Leader

John S. Nixon

Worship of the true God dominates salvation history from Eden to Patmos and remains as the central issue in the great controversy between Christ and Satan, as well as the number one priority in the life of the believer. A right relationship to Jesus Christ, which determines a relationship to everyone else in life, directly relates to one's spiritual condition, and nothing reveals a true spiritual condition like the beliefs, habits, and practices of the worship life. One can tell a lot about a church by observing its habits of worship, just as the life of personal devotion reflects the individual's spiritual life. For this reason, the pastor will always have a deep interest in the worship life of the individual member and of the church as a whole.

In its most basic formulation, worship may be defined as respect and reverence offered to a divine being or supernatural power. The root of the word has to do with *worth,* and worship's one true impetus recognizes the inherent worthiness of God apart from all other beings. The starting point of worship, therefore, does not center on the human condition but the divine reality. The focus of worship should not be my needs, my culture, or my emotional or intellectual expression. The true focus of worship is God Himself: God's attributes and perfections, God's glory and majesty, God's wisdom and will, God's words and deeds past, present, and future, toward the sons and daughters of men. Before He does anything that we can evaluate or even perceive, we recognize God as worthy of our highest devotion simply because He is God. After He has spoken and intervened and His actions are recognized by us as gracious, awesome, merciful, punitive, or even mysterious, He is still worthy of our highest devotion because He is God! The starting point of worship begins, not with the human condition, but the divine reality.

The arrangement of the camp of Israel during the wilderness years reflects the priority that worship should have in the believer's life. Whenever Israel pitched camp, the tabernacle was always at the center. Immediately beside it was the place of the priests, and a little farther out, that of the Levites, who also ministered in the tabernacle. Beyond the priests and Levites were all the tribes of Israel with their tents facing the place of worship.[1] There was never any doubt from the camp's configuration that the nation built its communal life around God. The political and social conventions of the nation also reflected the sovereign importance of the worship of God. In Hebrew society, a man could join the army at the age of twenty; a Levite could begin his sacred work in the temple at the age of twenty-five; but to take up the priesthood, a man had to be at least thirty years of age (Numbers 1:3; 8:24; 4:3). Nothing was more important to the expression of what it meant to be a citizen of Israel than worship.

Worship stays as the central issue over which the great controversy began in heaven and will conclude here on earth. Lucifer's ambition was, " 'I will raise my throne / above the stars of God; / I will sit enthroned on the mount of the assembly, . . . / I will make myself like the Most High' " (Isaiah 14:13, 14, NIV). He fell from his exalted position and lost his place in heaven because he coveted what belonged only to God. When the controversy reached earth, the first human casualty was Abel, who lost his life over the issue of worship. Cain killed his brother because Abel's offering was acceptable to God, while his own offering was not. And in the final test, soon to burst upon the church, the issue will again be worship with a choice between the mark of the beast and the seal of God. Worship shows what our lives are truly based on and a wise spiritual leader will recognize its importance.

The pastor's responsibility

If salvation history reveals the importance of worship, it also shows the necessity of pastoral leadership in worship and a matter of utmost importance for the edification and salvation of the church. Every time the people of God have fallen into false worship, poor spiritual leadership has been at the center. It was Aaron's weakness that led to the building of the golden calf at Sinai, resulting in the destruction of three thousand souls in one day. When the sanctuary worship degenerated in Israel during Samuel's time, the apostasy of Eli's sons, Hophni and Phineas, was at the root of the cause. And the corrupt worship practices that led Jesus to take a whip of cords and drive the money changers out of the temple could never have developed in the first place if the priests had not given in to the temptation to greed.[2]

With spiritual leadership critical to both the establishment and development of healthy corporate worship, pastors must not shrink from their responsibility in this matter. Ellen White gives important council in this regard: "Unless correct ideas of true worship and true reverence are impressed upon the people, there will be a growing tendency to place the sacred and eternal on a level with common things, and those professing the truth will be an offense to God and a disgrace to religion."[3]

"When a church has been raised up and left uninstructed on these points, the minister has neglected his duty and will have to give an account to God for the impressions he allowed to prevail."[4]

From this statement, we can clearly see the importance of the pastor being fully aware of the church's worship habits and their basis and to have a thorough understanding of what true worship is meant to be. With such an understanding, pastors will be able to instruct and guide the people of God as they formulate worship based on sound biblical principles.

The priority of worship in Adventist history

The strongest shared sense of identity held by the pioneers of the Seventh-day Adventist Church was that of mission. Early Adventists viewed themselves as having been "set in the world as watchmen and light bearers . . . given a work of the most solemn import—the proclamation of the first, second, and third angels' messages."[5] Because of the emphasis on true worship in these messages, particularly that of the first and third angels (Revelation 14:7, 9, 10), this awareness set an immediate priority for the early Advent believers. Adventists have always taken worship practice seriously and considered it integral to the success of the church's mission to make disciples of all nations (Matthew 28:19).

This issue was so crucial in early Adventist thought that the pioneers first considered *Holiness* as a name for their fledgling church because of its emphasis on the true spirit of worship. They finally settled on *Seventh-day Adventist* because it expressed in more detail the unique mission of the movement.[6] However, this should not be taken as a departure from the emphasis on worship, since the spiritual meaning of the Sabbath is *holiness* and the highest expression of Sabbath keeping has always been the gathering of the people in the house of God on the day set apart as holy. As the worship leader for the local church, the Adventist pastor will be in touch with this historic priority.

The true center of worship

In order to function as a worship leader, the minister must understand what is at the center of true worship. This has become a matter of contentious debate in modern religious circles, particularly when secular values have been permitted to slip in and compromise the principles at the root of worship. Strong arguments have been made for worship as a form of self-expression based on culture, emotion, intellect, ritual, or personal therapy needs, among others. Whatever the rationale and however distinct one form of expression may be from another, they all share the common basis of being anthropocentric, worship that originates from the human perspective, from the worshiper's perception of his own need. This may be compatible with the philosophy of the world, but it does not comport with the principles of Scripture.

In the cultural philosophy of the first century, the concept of freedom was highly individualized. Freedom was interpreted as personal power, the right of the individual to be free from outward constraint. At the height of the Roman Empire, the Roman citizen could travel anywhere in the world completely without fear. He knew that the mightiest nation in the world would defend his individual rights against all enemies.

The modern notion of freedom in Western culture has the same basis. Americans believe that freedom is expressed in the right of individuals to do as they please, a value deeply rooted in the Western mind that we will defend to the death. The West interprets personal freedom as a divine right based on natural law but does not take into account the New Testament's reinterpretation of freedom based on the Christ event. And without realizing it, the church has bought into the world's misunderstanding. Worship has been co-opted in the cause of personal freedom as a form of personality projection as expressed in the American Idol syndrome: "I have a testimony, I have a song, I have a word of wisdom. Let me be seen. Let me be heard. Let me get my praise on!" Somewhere in the haze of political and popular values, the church has lost much of the spiritual priority of worship and the task of the pastor as worship leader includes helping the church get it back.

True worship of the true God should not be viewed as a matter of personal freedom or self-expression of any kind. In fact, it is not about self-seeking at all, or therapy for me, or my own cultural outlet, or a platform for the display of my talents and abilities. Worship is the act of giving to God what God alone is due, willingly and lovingly in response to all He has given and constantly gives to me. True spiritual worship means to receive the mind of Christ and to conform my mind to His mind,[7] to bring myself into perfect submission to Christ that His life may be exhibited in mine. I come to know God this way, and now my entire life becomes an expression of worship at all times, described as the object of presenting myself to God in worship. Worship based on God means that God is both the Source and goal of everything I think and do. Inevitably, this kind of worship leads to a selfless life lived for others to the glory of God.

The thoughts of the mind are meant to dwell on God in worship, not on self. The by-product of this intentional other focus results in my needs being met in my meeting with God, including the deep inner needs of which I am not even aware. Whatever I think of God, God is greater than I think and worthy of my highest devotion without any self-interest or self-seeking mixed in. When we, by faith, forget ourselves in worship and give God His due, we, in turn, receive blessings in the process. God knows how to love us and take care of us, and He can be trusted to supply our needs when we abandon ourselves to Him. The spirit of self-abandonment in worship fosters the spirit of loving service for others so that the worshiper becomes the embodiment of the ministry of Christ on the earth, which was lived for the "least of these."

Every song, every prayer, every spoken word, and even our silence in worship becomes an offering to the One who fills our hearts and minds so that no room can be found for self. Every fellowship among us as worshipers, every stitch of clothing we put on, every gesture, posture, motive, and thought comes from God and goes back to God from a humble, contrite, and adoring heart. With no need to manufacture hoopla to show that my worship isn't boring, there is no need for applause to certify that what I have to offer in worship is worthwhile; and no need for congratulations from my fellow worshipers so that my ego will not be bruised. We do not need to be personally noticed at all, since, in worship as in life, Jesus Christ is all in all.

Principles of worship practice for the church

With the true basis of worship clearly in view, the pastor may now set principles upon which specific worship practices may be built. These principles will serve as the foundation for worship in the various corporate gatherings of the church, Sabbath School, prayer meeting, and the divine worship service. They will have their basis in Scripture and reflect the important emphasis of worship from the top down, not the bottom up, in other words, worship that begins with the divine reality and prerogatives as revealed in Scripture, not with the human condition or human felt needs. In this way, worship will find its goal and purpose in the sole objective of pleasing God, which objective alone leads to the highest human satisfaction and fulfillment as the worshiper receives the gracious approbation of the One being worshiped. The principles that will form the basis of worship development, along with some guidelines for implementation, follow.

1. Proclamation. As the central act of corporate worship, proclamation can be described as the preaching and teaching of the everlasting gospel of Jesus Christ as the central act of corporate worship. Proclamation based on Scripture is the foundational and climactic act of worship around which other liturgical acts are built. The idea includes the presentation of the final-hour message that the Adventist Church has been especially commissioned to present. Proclamation, while not limited to the formal sermon alone, however, may also include a variety of communication forms and formats, all of which seek to expose and apply from the Bible God's meaning in Christ under the guidance of the Holy Spirit.

In this understanding, the New Testament sacraments of footwashing, the Lord's Supper, and baptism come under the heading of proclamation. They serve as visible signs of the Word of God proclaimed and apprehended by the believer based on faith. Not meant to replace the verbal proclamation of the Word, since "faith comes by hearing," these sacraments only supplement it so as to make it more accessible to the worshiper.[8] As proclamation from the standpoint of Adventist mission, the preaching and teaching of the Word in worship will have an evangelistic intent built on the final warning message and appeal to spiritual renewal—an integral part of Adventist eschatology (Revelation 14:6–12).

2. Corporate prayer. As the opening of the heart to God as to a friend, prayer brings the worshipers together into personal contact with the Almighty. Along with praise, thanksgiving, confession, and petition, corporate prayer includes the sacred trust of mutual *intercession* by believers on each other's behalf (Ephesians 6:18). This important aspect of communal prayer will be all the more critical in a community with significant generational or cultural differences. Intercessory prayer needs to be encouraged across generational and cultural lines without engendering the guilt of fear that would make prayer something other than voluntary, and therefore, something less than genuine.

Communal intercessory prayer may be modeled on the example of the early Christian church as described in passages such as Acts 4:24–26 and Acts 12:5. The understanding of intercession and the desire to participate in it will be developed by the pastor in other areas of corporate life that present the opportunity for instruction and relationship building, such as Bible study, prayer meeting, testimony services, and even personal, one-on-one communication.

3. Participation. As an act of the entire community, corporate worship calls for every-member participation with understanding and fullness of heart (Ephesians 5:19, 20). In worship centered in proclamation, the danger always exists that worshipers will become spectators who gather each week for a preaching event. Other liturgical acts may even be viewed as routine, necessary preliminaries to be expended as quickly as possible so as to make room for the main event. Preachers may come to be viewed as performers whose pulpit reputations become the drawing card for worship and the main attraction of the service. To avoid these distortions, which take away from the focus on God, congregational participation in worship must be fostered. Some of the ways in which this may be done include the following:

- Build the worship service around the music of congregational singing instead of special selections by the choir or guest musicians.
- Include members of all ages in the lineup of liturgical participants from week to week.
- Integrate into the worship service testimonies from worshipers of all ages who have had personal experiences with divine intervention in their lives.
- Arrange for families to lead out as a unit in the congregational prayer or Scripture reading, or some other element of worship.
- Employ the small-group prayer gathering in which members are encouraged to share prayer needs with each other in a circle of prayer.
- Institute the "family on the altar" service in which entire families are brought before the church, introduced to the congregation

one by one, and then prayed for by the pastor or worship leader, along with the congregation.

- Use responsive readings in worship that may be read from the Bible or other books, or projected on a screen for worshipers to read in unison.

4. Praise. Worship that begins with God cannot be devoid of the heartfelt praise that a realization of the divine grace and majesty always prompts. This will be spontaneous and free, as the Spirit of God moves the worshipers, but it may also be ordered and planned, as in the songs of praise offered to God by choir and congregation (1 Corinthians 14:15). In order for communal praise to be edifying, however, it must be genuine, and in order for it to be genuine it must be welcome without being required. Respect must be given for the differences in temperament, experience, culture, and age that will have an effect on the way individuals express themselves in the public setting of corporate worship.

The praise of God in communal worship should always be a response to God and to God's activities and should never degenerate into a mere effect meant to create a sense of excitement. Not only does such an emphasis in worship shift the primary focus from the divine to the human, it also tends to create a reliance on emotional expression as the sign of genuine spirituality. Laugh tracks and applause signs belong to the sitcom and the studio. The response of the worshiper to the acts of God should be prompted by the Holy Spirit and no one else.

5. Reverence. With a deep appreciation for the holy "otherness" of God, corporate worship will exemplify the reverence and awe that always distinguishes the sacred from the profane (1 Timothy 6:15, 16). While not meant as a contradiction to the expression of praise previously mentioned, the kind of praise appropriate to worship will be characterized by reverence and awe. In some communities, careful instruction will need to be given regarding the observance of reverence in worship. The holy transcendence of God as an aspect of the divine nature, along with God's immanence as the One who is always near, may be taught in the church's gathering times for instruction. In order for reverence to be heartfelt and sincere, not just mandated and enforced, worshipers need to understand and appreciate the awesomeness of God as different and distant from us but at the same time, intimate and near to the one who trusts in Him. Prayer and instruction will combine to create in the congregation an appreciation for this divine paradox.

6. Generosity. With the reality of spiritual oneness in view, corporate worship also calls for the giving of oneself to Christ and to people in ways including the rendering of material gifts (1 Timothy 6:17–19). The believers' consciousness of themselves as members of a worldwide community will open their eyes to the vast field of need. As the worship leader, the pastor should emphasize the communal obligations incumbent upon every believer, who must understand the principle of stewardship and how it differs from capitalism. While the capitalist may cling to concepts of private property and discretionary money, stewards realize they are not the outright owners of anything in their possession. God alone owns the earth and everything in it, including every person, and stewards of the Most High God will consider it an honor to be able to give what has been entrusted to them where it is needed.

7. Fellowship. In full discernment of the significance of Christ's body as the kingdom of God on earth, corporate worship should take the time for recognition between fellow worshipers. In the context of the body of Christ, this will be more than a social convention, but an expression of deep love for those whom Jesus has made one with Himself (Ephesians 4:28; 1 Thessalonians 5:11). Fellowship in worship gives the opportunity for members to further bond with one another, not as mere acquaintances or friends, but as brothers and sisters in Christ. The pastor who understands the essential nature of the church as an organism, not just an organization, will want the membership to experience all stages of relationships that lead to bonding.

Many of the activities suggested in this section, particularly under the prayer and participation headings, will also enhance the fellowship aspect of communal worship. In addition to these, however, the pastor may wish to encourage a brief time of reverent greeting between worshipers as an integral part of worship. Careful instruction with regard to the meaning of Christian community will alleviate concerns some may harbor that greeting fellow worshipers somehow disrespects the presence of God.

God desires that His people should be changed through the correct practice of worship. True worship is meant to have a continuing and permanent impact on the life, not just a temporary one to lead to holy living (Isaiah 1:10–18). Pastors as worship leaders will be effective for God only as they give up worship to divine control. While the pastor may be the director of worship, they should not be considered the producer. God alone is both the Source and the goal of everything having to do with true worship.

---

1. John MacArthur Jr., *The Ultimate Priority* (Chicago: Moody Press, 1983), 3.

2. See Exodus 32; 1 Samuel 2; and Matthew 21.

3. White, *Testimonies for the Church,* 5:500.

4. Ibid.

5. White, *Testimonies for the Church,* 9:19.

6. J. N. Loughborough, *Rise and Progress of the Seventh-day Adventists* (Battle Creek, MI: General Conference Association, 1892), 221.

7. Oswald Chambers, "March 30," *My Utmost for His Highest: Selections for the Year* (Grand Rapids, MI: Discovery House Publishers, 1993).

8. See Romans 10:17.

Chapter 7

The Pastor as Preacher-Evangelist

Abraham J. Jules

Introduction

The pastor as preacher-evangelist stands in a long tradition of "the oral transmission of the Word of God as gospel from the heart and mind of the preacher to the hearts and minds of the people."[1] Throughout history, preaching has played a significant role in the work of God's people. Noah, commissioned by God to warn the antediluvian world of imminent danger, carries the description of "a preacher of righteousness" (2 Peter 2:5, KJV). Isaiah and Jeremiah were not only prophets but preachers as well. Indeed, the earliest Gospel, Mark, makes the poignant point that "Jesus came into Galilee, *preaching* the gospel of the kingdom of God" (1:14, KJV; italics supplied; cf. Matthew 4:17). With the mission of the last-day church to preach the everlasting gospel (Revelation 14:6), the preacher in the twenty-first century simply carries on the mission of the Master.

The importance of preaching

God called Jonah to go to Nineveh and preach to its inhabitants according to the divine directives (Jonah 3:2). In the New Testament, preaching receives special significance: John the Baptist and Jesus came preaching, the Day of Pentecost is known for the Spirit-filled preaching of Peter, and the book of Acts is filled with preaching. Further, God has chosen to use the "foolishness of preaching" (1 Corinthians 1:21, KJV) to save the lost. As a pastor-evangelist, Paul described himself as a preacher and apostle (1 Timothy 2:7, KJV) and charged the young pastor Timothy, "*Preach* the Word; be instant in season, out of season; . . . do the work of an *evangelist,* make full proof of thy ministry" (2 Timothy 4:2–5, KJV; italics supplied). Paul says explicitly that the work of the minister involves preaching and evangelism. The same duty devolves upon us several centuries later so that, "the work of the pastor is summed up in the pulpit."[2]

The need for awareness

C. Sumner Wemp reminds us that not only mature Christians may have opportunity to listen to our preaching. The unsaved, babes in Christ, and carnal Christians may also hear.[3] Hence, in a way, all preaching is evangelistic in nature because the goal includes bringing people to, and growing them in Christ. In my twenty-three years of ministry, I have been careful to ensure that as a pastor all my preaching calls people to both renewal and conversion. In short, pastors must be aware of their dual role as preacher and evangelist.

Richard Stoll Armstrong puts its well:

> To the unchurched in the congregation, the preacher must be an evangelist. For those who are already members of the church, the task is renewal and the preacher literally speaking is more of a revivalist. Both groups need to hear the gospel, but their different relationships to the church call for differences in the preacher's appeal for decision. Evangelism and revivalism are related but different, and the pastor-evangelist is sensitive to the differences as well as the similarities. The pastor-evangelist as preacher is therefore both an evangelist and a revivalist, always striving to communicate to the unchurched as well as to the flock.[4]

The need for urgency

When a potential disciple of Jesus requested to first bury his dead father and then follow Him, Jesus replied, "Let the dead bury their dead: but go thou and *preach* the kingdom of God" (Luke 9:60, KJV; italics supplied). He placed the emphasis on the urgency of carrying the gospel. This same premium on preaching also occurs in the Great Commission (Matthew 28:18–20). Here Jesus engages His followers for all time in the "imperative indicative."[5] Three significant factors are brought to light in this passage:

1. Authority (Matthew 28:18). The Greek word *exousia* speaks of the power of authority with Jesus invested with this universal authority, and believers given similar authority (John 1:12). This translates into raw power (*dunamis*) for the purpose of carrying the gospel (Acts 1:8). Luke 9:1, 2 illustrates this. He (Jesus) called the Twelve and gave them power (*dunamis*) and authority (*exousia*) over all demons and to cure diseases, and He sent them out to *preach* the kingdom of God and to heal.

2. Assignment (Matthew 28:19, 20a). Our duty includes teaching/preaching what Jesus commands. Some contemporary scholars make an ill-fated effort to differentiate between preaching and teaching in the New Testament. But as pastors know from experience, both constitute one and the same thing because the subject of both is the same—Jesus Christ. While teaching may point in the direction of instruction and preaching to proclamation, no one can argue that both are not deeply interwoven: the pastor teaches invaluable truths in the signal act of preaching. Acts 5:42 underlines this: "Day after day, in the temple courts and from house to house, they never stopped teaching and proclaiming the good news that Jesus is the Christ" (NIV).

3. Assurance (Matthew 28:20b). Jesus promised, " 'And surely I am with you always, to the very end of the age' " (NIV). Besides this commission, the New Testament places focus on the urgency of preaching in several other places: Matthew 10:7, 27; Mark 16:15; Luke 9:2; Acts 5:20; Romans 10:13–15; 2 Timothy 4:2. Pastors today need to study these and with each preaching event they must be moved with the "urgency of its appeal," realizing it must have a "once-for-all, now-or-never, all-or-nothing, either-or quality."[6] This is the essence of Richard Baxter's well-known injunction, "Preach as a dying man to dying men."

The need for authority

David Fisher, senior pastor of Colonial Church in Edina, Minnesota, United States, laments the crisis of authority both in the church and the wider society and concludes, "The cultural conflict and resistance to authority in our time make *pastoral ministry increasingly difficult*."[7] In light of this, he calls for a resurgence of the preaching authority of the pastor. He says forcefully,

> In no area is authority more significant for pastoral ministry than in preaching for it is in the pulpit that we speak the Word of Christ. The tone of our leadership is set in the moral and spiritual authority we model in our preaching. Preaching is the public demonstration that the Word of God is at work in us, and it is the tool that God uses to speak to the church and the world. Preaching without authority robs the Word of God of its essence; it is like an army without weapons. The gospel of Christ demands the authority inherent in it.[8]

We are called "to preach" (*ke͞russo͞*), literally to cry out or proclaim as a herald. In the New Testament world, the herald was the spokesperson for the royal court and bore the dignity of the same because he was backed by the authority of the king. Such authority is invested in the preacher as an ambassador—the duly appointed representative of their government while working in a foreign field. Pastor Paul, the preacher-evangelist, was keenly aware that his critics in Corinth could oppose but not depose him because he spoke with the dignity, power, and authority of Christ the King (2 Corinthians 5:20). Indeed, our authority is derived from the plain "Thus says the Lord."

The need for the Spirit in our preaching

Preachers must be filled with the Holy Spirit in order to preach effectively. If not, their work does not constitute "a word from God" but a mere speech that echoes human reflection on the Scriptures. Undoubtedly, at times this may follow well the rules of homiletics, founded in sound exegesis and powerful oral presentation; but without the convicting power of the accompanying Holy Spirit, it bears the cacophony of "a resounding gong or a clanging cymbal" (1 Corinthians 13:1, NIV).

The value of the Holy Spirit is underscored in Jesus' Messianic declaration in Luke 4:16–21. At its core (verses 18, 19, KJV; quoting Isaiah 61:1, 2) is highlighted the unmistakable relationship between preaching and the Spirit: "The Spirit of the Lord is upon me, because he hath anointed me to *preach* the gospel to the poor; . . . to *preach* deliverance to the captives . . . To *preach* the acceptable year of the Lord" (italics supplied). Commenting on the overall significance of this passage and the call to be pervasive and purposeful in proclaiming the gospel, J. H. Jowett, the former pastor of Fifth Avenue Presbyterian Church of New York, said in his Yale lectures on preaching that in this Spirit-filled preaching "there is the sound of the song of freedom."[9] In light of this, we must follow the Master in His mission accomplished in "two ways: by the service of good news and by the good news of service."[10]

To be certain, greatness in the pulpit does not come in intellectual greatness or silver-tongued eloquence; rather, the preacher as the medium of God's message must pay attention to Charles E. Bradford's counsel to leave "room . . . for the Spirit to lead."[11]

The need for Christ-centered preaching

All too often, especially in evangelistic preaching, the emphasis is overly placed on doctrine. Although I, too, believe that every sermon should have some doctrinal orientation that illuminates a biblical truth,[12] we cannot highlight the law, Sabbath, and state of the dead and others, while ignoring the centrality of Christ in our preaching.

Sometimes we find it all too easy to draw attention to ourselves by the dramatics of preaching. While this may titillate the admiration of listeners, it does not win hearts to Christ. Only as we lift Him up will *all* people be drawn to Him (John 12:32). This was the singular mission of Jesus, and the twenty-first-century preacher must emulate this mission—Christ-centered preaching that declares inclusive emancipation. We do well to follow the examples of the apostles in the first century who focused on Christ:

"Then Philip went down to the city of Samaria, and preached Christ unto them" (Acts 8:5, KJV).

"Then Philip opened his mouth, and began at the same scripture, and preached unto him Jesus" (Acts 8:35, KJV).

"And straightway he preached Christ in the synagogues, that he is the Son of God" (Acts 9:20, KJV).

"This Jesus, whom I preach unto you, is Christ" (Acts 17:3b, KJV).

"But we preach Christ crucified, unto the Jews a stumblingblock, and unto the Greeks foolishness" (1 Corinthians 1:23, KJV).

"For we preach not ourselves, but Christ Jesus the Lord" (2 Corinthians 4:5, KJV).

The need for a Christlike passion for souls

The pastor who invests time, energy, and effort in preaching must not be motivated by ambitions such as impressing peers and superiors or the drive to satisfy the desire for success by baptizing many people or the need to lead or lord it over large congregations. The pastor must be compelled by "a Christ-like burden for lost souls."[13] Indeed, "The lost get saved when the found get burdened."[14] When this happens, our evangelistic preaching becomes even more concentrated. In this light, Wemp outlines five principles that will enhance our preaching:

1. Create an atmosphere for evangelism in your church.
2. Encourage your people to bring the unsaved to church.
3. Invite the unsaved to come.
4. Put the gospel in every message and give the unsaved an opportunity to be saved.

5. Teach your people to pray, and expect people to be saved.[15]

The need for relevance

Charles E. Bradford, the outstanding preacher-evangelist and former president of the North American Division of Seventh-day Adventists, often remarks that the preacher must have the Bible in one hand and the newspaper in the other. The point, of course, is that the preacher must be relevant. "As he shapes and fashions his message, which is based on eternal truth, the preacher must ask what the contemporary mind is. What are the ideas and ideologies that mold and motivate people today? It is in the light of these questions that he benefits from knowledge of current events, history, psychology, sociology and the findings of science in all of its disciplines."[16]

Carnegie S. Calian echoes a similar sentiment when he comments that theology that refuses to "wrestle with life issues is not worthy of people's attention in the marketplace."[17]

The need for reflection

The experience of over two decades of ministry has taught me three important principles on which the pastor as preacher-evangelist must reflect.

1. Prayer. The busyness of a pastor's life could often eclipse the need for prayer, reflection, and study. But precisely because of such duties they must invest time in dedicated prayer. "Learn to pray before you learn to preach, and you will preach with power."[18] After all, "Prayer moves the arm of Omnipotence."[19]

2. Passion. This heightens our sense of urgency in preaching the gospel. "Passion is essential to preaching. . . . The hearer should know that here, clearly, is a person urgently trying to communicate something that is important to him."[20]

3. Partnership with God. Listen to the voice of God in His Word and surrender all your assets to Him, such that you do not depend on your abilities. The Word of God must burn in your own heart first (Jeremiah 20:9) so that it may burn within others (Luke 24:32).

1. Charles E. Bradford, *Preaching to the Times: The Preaching Ministry in the Seventh-day Adventist Church* (Silver Spring, MD: Ministerial Association, General Conference of Seventh-day Adventists, n.d.), 39.

2. David Fisher, *The 21st Century Pastor: A Vision Based on the Ministry of Paul* (Grand Rapids, MI: Zondervan, 1996), 242.

3. C. Sumner Wemp, *The Guide to Practical Pastoring* (Nashville: Thomas Nelson, 1982), 210.

4. Richard Stoll Armstrong, *The Pastor-Evangelist in Worship* (Philadelphia: Westminster, 1986), 110.

5. Richard John Neuhaus, *Freedom for Ministry* (New York: Harper & Row, 1979), 185–207.

6. Armstrong, *The Pastor-Evangelist,* 117.

7. Fisher, *The 21st Century Pastor,* 231; italics supplied.

8. Ibid., 234.

9. J. H. Jowett, *The Preacher: His Life and Work* (Garden City, NY: Doubleday, Doran & Co., 1928), 32.

10. Ibid., 33.

11. Bradford, *Preaching to the Times,* 35.

12. Ibid., 49.

13. Michael J. Fox and Joe Samuel Ratliff, *Church Planting in the African American Community* (Valley Forge, PA: Judson, 2002), 45.

14. Wemp, *Guide to Practiced Pastoring,* 175.

15. Ibid., 176.

16. Bradford, *Preaching to the Times,* 13, 14.

17. Carnegie S. Calian, *Today's Pastor in Tomorrow's World,* rev. ed. (Philadelphia: Westminster, 1982), 42.

18. Wemp, *Guide to Practical Pastoring,* 212.

19. White, *Christ's Object Lessons,* 172.

20. Richard John Neuhaus, *Freedom for Ministry,* rev. ed. (Grand Rapids, MI: Eerdmans, 1992), 172.

Chapter 8

The Pastor as an Administrator

Adrian Craig

A Methodist minister put it this way: " 'The modern preacher has to make as many visits as a country doctor, shake as many hands as a politician, prepare as many briefs as a lawyer, and see as many people as a specialist. He has to be as good an executive as the president of a university, as good a financier as a bank president; and in the midst of it all, he has to be so good a diplomat that he could umpire a baseball game between the Knights of Columbus and the Ku Klux Klan.' "[1]

You are never to do everything, but you are to attempt to see that everything is done. That describes administration in the pastorate—you are responsible for the implementation and operation of the church program. Capable of arranging, setting in order, and putting members to work, the pastor oversees the functioning of the church.

By definition, *administration* is "ad-minister"—something that happens prior to ministry or serving—something added to make ministry work. As pastor, you are to see that the various departments, services, committees, and boards function. You need to be present at the major church committees and receive reports from the various committees detailing their activity. You will want to meet with the various leaders of your church and see that each officer has a clearly defined responsibility sheet or job description. Function happens best when officers know what is expected, so a flow chart outlining levels of responsibility and to whom officers are responsible is vital.

Skills in chairing committees

As a pastor-administrator, make sure skills in chairing committees are learned and developed. The pastor, or a qualified layperson, should chair the major committee/boards of the church. This individual should know committee procedure, understand parliamentary process, and know, for example, what is meant by main motions, preferential motions, amendments, and optional methods of voting. They should study the committee agenda, understand the issues behind the agenda items, and allow appropriate time for discussion. The chairperson directs the traffic, controls the flow, and lets the committee be the true conscience for the church. Unnecessary and lengthy discussion on matters of minor consequence should be discouraged. The chairperson must know the difference between processes, functions, policies, and procedures, and know the *Church Manual*.

Your shepherding style becomes very evident in committee work, so you'll need to promote a participatory style, and know what items go on which agenda. The committee agenda must relate to the terms of reference for that committee. With an issue beyond immediate resolve, table the item for a subsequent meeting to allow more time for reflection and prayer.

As an effective administrator, the pastor respects the sisterhood of churches, the administration process, and structure of the church. Interchurch harmony is encouraged and leadership honored. The great miracle of grace demonstrates that varied dispositions, cultures, academic backgrounds, ethnicity, along with gender and age variations, in no way impedes our Master's desire for His church as expressed in His priestly prayer of John 17 "to be one."

Administration should not be for dominance, lordship, or dictatorship. The pastor's administrative style contributes to the health and vitality of the church. A *well* church has leadership that empowers, considers all members as key players of the team, and ensures they are adequately trained and tutored in their role. The pastor will be people-oriented, working in partnership with the team as player/coach. The Master model is the pastor's model: " 'Just as the Son of Man did not come to be served, but to serve' " (Matthew 20:28, NIV; see also Matthew 20:25–27).

If, as a pastor, you immerse yourself in all the functions of the church, you are inviting fatigue and burnout. To stop this, see that all sections of the church are working, and you will then be able to maximize ministry time in the key areas of preaching, mission, and nurture. Frustrated pastors, unfulfilled pastors, and pastors lacking empowerment become such because of the minimizing of their key roles. A plumber who never plumbs, a pilot who never flies, a baker who never bakes, and a surgeon who never operates are frustrated.

While at times some lesser roles must be on the pastoral agenda, one must refrain from majoring in minors. Biblical counsel is imperative on this point. Moses was wearing himself out doing everything when his father-in-law counseled him to divide responsibility and appoint leaders over thousands, hundreds, and tens.[2] In the New Testament, the apostolic church was in danger because vital ministerial function was threatened. "So the Twelve gathered all the disciples together and said, 'It would not be right for us to neglect the ministry of the word of God in order to wait on tables' " (Acts 6:2, NIV). Deacons were selected to assist in the routine church duties.[3]

Study the chapter in *Gospel Workers,* by Ellen G. White, on "A Division of Labor," pages 196–200. In this chapter, Ellen White gives an illustration of a company owner who discovered his foreman busy doing the work of his team, while they stood idly by. The company owner made the foreman redundant because he said that he employed the foreman to keep six others busy, but they were idle while the foreman was busy. He could not pay the wages of seven for the foreman to teach six how to be idle.

" 'But many pastors fail in not knowing how, or in not trying, to get the full membership of the church actively engaged in the various departments of church work. If pastors would give more attention to getting and keeping their flock actively engaged at work, they would accomplish more good, have more time for study and religious visiting, and also avoid many causes of friction.' "[4]

Working church—growing church

Ellen White indicated that a working church becomes a growing church. The Adventist Church grows best with the minimizing of unemployment and the maximizing of involvement in the life of the church. Jesus gave this message loud and clear in His final sermon on the mount in Matthew 24 and 25. In Matthew 25, He tells the church that the most dangerous time is the waiting time, living in expectation of a long-awaited Advent. The Jews missed the First Advent, so the end-time church must be on full alert to be ready for the Second Advent. The foolish virgins missed out on the kingdom because they were religious spectators. They were not in the field, at the workplace, doing the business of the church. Vitality and readiness are only maintained by active participation in church life. The parable of the talents follows the parable of the virgins to show us how to wait. Waiting is not passive but active. "Where there is no active labor for others, love wanes, and faith grows dim."[5]

Pastoral priority involves administering the Word, and neglecting it takes away the life of the church. The apostles in Acts 6 put the church to work so their work of ministering the Word would be realized. Because you are God's mouthpiece, you will need to spend time preparing to deliver a biblical message.

Many people are crying out for a word from the Father. They are interested in music, but they may not be hungry for that or even for prayer. They want to know what the Father has spoken. In a world of fashion and change and a multitude of false voices pressing for a listening ear, people want to know what the true authority—God's Word—says.[6]

A radical shift

"A new way of 'doing' church is emerging. In this radical paradigm shift exposition is being replaced with entertainment, preaching with performances, doctrine with drama, and theology with theatrics. The pulpit, once the focal point of the church, is now being overshadowed by a variety of church-growth techniques, everything from trendy worship styles to glitzy presentations to vaudeville-like pageantries. In seeking to capture the upper hand in church growth, a new wave of pastors is reinventing church and repackaging the gospel into a product to be sold to 'consumers.' "[7]

Paul's counsel to Timothy needs to be read every day by the pastor: "Challenge, warn, and urge your people. Don't ever quit. Just keep it simple. You're going to find that there will be times when people will have no stomach for solid teaching, but will fill up on spiritual junk food—catchy opinions that tickle their fancy. They'll turn their backs on truth and chase mirages. But you—keep your eye on what you are doing; accept the hard times along with the good; keep the Message alive; do a thorough job as God's servant."[8]

Uplift Christ

Preach Adventist sermons. Christ-centred, Bible-based sermons feed the people. Vary the menu and give the full, complete Adventist menu. Never should a sermon be preached without uplifting the One who will draw, attract, and appeal to all. Preach the full Adventist gospel—the Bible gospel that justifies, sanctifies, and glorifies; that which deals with the penalty, power, and presence of sin that balances law and gospel, for graceless law is legalism and lawless grace is licentiousness. "The law is the gospel embodied, and the gospel is the law unfolded."[9]

Preach from the Old and New Testaments. Preach prophecy. Preach an Adventist Christ-centred lifestyle. Preach the Second Advent. Preach Adventist family and home. Preach a series on Daniel and Revelation, justification by faith, and the home. Preach topically and on books of the Bible. Use visiting preachers to supplement your presentations for a Week of Prayer series or evangelistic meetings. Attend seminars on preaching. If there are no seminars available, request your conference leadership to arrange one presented by a pulpit master. Read about preaching and listen to giants of preaching. "When we eat Christ's flesh and drink His blood, the element of eternal life will be found in the ministry. There will be not be a fund of stale, oft-repeated ideas. The tame, dull sermonizing will cease. The old truths will be presented, but they will be seen in a new light. There will be a new perception of truth, a clearness and a power that all will discern."[10]

Jesus says, " 'Therefore every teacher of the law who has been instructed about the kingdom of heaven is like the owner of a house who brings out of his storeroom new treasures as well as old' " (Matthew 13:52, NIV).

"The world will not be converted by the gift of tongues, or by the working of miracles, but by preaching Christ crucified."[11] "If those who today are teaching the word of God, would uplift the cross of Christ higher still higher, their ministry would be far more successful."[12]

Administer mission. Teach the saints how to witness with every church as a training school for outreach. "God has not given His ministers the work of setting the churches right. No sooner is this work done, apparently, than it has to be done over again. Church members that are thus looked after and labored for become religious weaklings. If nine tenths of the effort that has been put forth for those who know the truth had been put forth for those who had never heard the truth, how much greater would have been the advancement made!"[13] "Training is the best nurture that can be given to God's people, but nurture for the sake of nurture only embeds people more deeply into Laodicean indifference."[14]

Ellen White identifies the one-talent person with the person who has drifted along doing nothing for the church—idly standing by in the marketplace waiting for assignment. She says, "They love to hear the gospel preached, and therefore think themselves Christians. . . . Like the Jews, they mistake the enjoyment of their blessings for the use they should make of them. . . .

". . . The continual misuse of their talents will effectually quench for them the Holy Spirit."[15]

Administer nurture. All families with their different needs are to be cared for. The elders are shepherds and membership/attendance lists need to be given to this team because their assignment includes caring for the members. Deacons and deaconesses also have a shepherding role. In a large church, the pastoral team cannot and should not do all the visiting, for members should also care for members. At your monthly elders' meetings, review the shepherding these individuals have done, and keep briefed on significant membership concerns. The pastor must maintain personal membership contact to be able to address from the pulpit the perplexities and pain of those in the pew.

In your nurturing role, you will have to deal with differences of opinion or conflict at various levels. Conflict should not necessarily be considered wrong, for the statement that when two minds are thinking alike one mind is not thinking at all, may have some truth. Because humanity has always been subjected to differences of opinion that impact relationships, planned, deliberate variance, for the sake of contention, is not healthy either. Abraham's and Lot's herdsmen debated as to who was greatest in the disciple team. John and James's request for prominent kingdom positions caused strife. Paul and Barnabas had an argument over John Mark's place on the evangelistic team. The early church had dissention over the neglect of certain widows.

In addressing conflict, get the opposing parties together, and listen carefully to each point of view. Seek resolve from the parties themselves, and guide the discussion with biblical principles. Time is needed to resolve problems, particularly in cases where long-term conflict has existed and is charged with emotion. Maintain impartiality.

The Christian motivation for reconciliation and forgiveness should undergird all conflict resolution. While personally addressing conflict resolution, time will determine how much you immerse yourself in this aspect of nurture. A wise pastor will delegate in this area. A church with a larger membership may have a team of lay or professional people skilled in dealing with dissension.

The pastor should aim to be a master of diplomacy. In that electrically charged atmosphere of Thursday night in the upper room, Jesus dismantled all self-elevation by the high volume of deeds, not words. Action was highly audible and melted dissension. When Peter's turn came to have his feet washed, he strongly resisted. It was too humiliating to allow the Master to be the servant, but Jesus dismantled Peter's opposition, and His act of servanthood that removed alienation and strife was diplomacy at its best.

In dealing with Simon the Pharisee and Mary Magdalene, Jesus showed diplomacy, for He could effectively deal with both individuals.

He gave recognition to Mary for her charity that was questioned by the disciples, when He said, " 'She has done a beautiful thing to me' " (Mark 14:6, NIV). Jesus impressed Simon by not openly exposing him to the guests and then used a story to appeal to him. Simon was not treated as he wished Mary to be treated. Jesus, by compassion and conveyed concern, exposed Simon's heart to himself and the proud Pharisee fell on the Rock and was broken.

Study the Master Pastor to see how He resolved differences and melted stony hearts. Study Jesus' dealings with Peter, Judas, the Pharisees, and Thomas. Use Scripture and *The Desire of Ages* to carefully study Jesus' methods, and list all of Jesus' one-on-one encounters. Read Romans 12:16, 18 for Paul's counsel.

Administering nurture will give rise to the need for counseling, but differentiate between pastoral counseling and psychotherapy. The couch should never replace the pulpit. While psychology has become a valuable discipline to help understand the human mind and emotion, the pastor needs to be alert to the secular humanistic foundations of modern psychology and practice. Psychology, for ministerial purposes, must be tested by the queen of disciplines—theology—and psychology should be one of the tools to aid the pastor in nurturing. However, the therapeutic revolution must not be allowed to impact the church and to parade as the twenty-first-century messiah to heal humanity and interpret life.

"Psychological Man views the world and experiences life in psychological categories. Complexes, repressions, denials, inhibitions, obsessions, traumas and codependencies are far more 'real' than original sin or the image of God. As the devil complains in Jeremy Leven's novel *Satan*, 'Psychotherapy worries the hell out of me. . . . It keeps turning evil into neuroses and explaining away people's behaviour with drives and complexes. . . . Modern psychiatry is putting me out of business.' "[16]

Pastoral counseling should feature a one-on-one discussion on a particular matter of concern. As counselor, you may give advice or information, but the key approach is to listen, remembering that we have two ears and one mouth. Encourage the counselee to state clearly his or her problem and try to understand his or her emotion. Once the issue of concern has been made clear, the wise counselor graciously recites principles to assist the counselee in resolving his or her own concerns. Individual responsibility must never be abdicated and counselor dependency should be avoided.

"Man is genuinely responsible for his behaviour, as the Biblical doctrine of sin teaches, and pastoral counsellors must be on guard not to succumb to pressure to water down human responsibility. The answer is not to minimize sin, but rather to make forgiveness more operational. A therapy which gives the patient a combination of hormones and tranquilizers will not be enough, nor is it sufficient to gain insight into the forces that have moulded personality. Unless the client accepts his responsibility, he cannot truly experience the therapeutic release which true forgiveness brings."[17]

Counseling may be a nurturing role for a pastor but not the only role. The wise pastor knows the limitations on time and measures one's own skills. The pastor refers individuals to specialists for various reasons:

1. When there is serious emotional disturbance.
2. When there are within the membership or ministerial team persons trained in behavioral science—whose full-time work is to counsel.
3. When time management does not allow the effective pastor to deal with every member in distress and crisis.
4. When after a few sessions you have made no progress.
5. When there is an inability to isolate the problem.
6. When there is a chemical addiction.
7. When there is sexual perversion or abuse.

In all counseling within the church, promote confidentiality, set time limits on counseling sessions, and be careful with cross-gender counseling.

Conclusion

" 'The preacher for today must have the heart of a lion, the skin of a hippopotamus, the agility of a greyhound, the patience of a donkey, the wisdom of an elephant, the industry of an ant, and as many lives as a cat.' "[18] Pastors need many attributes and skills, but above all they are Jesus' representatives.

Pastors are the spiritual leaders of the church, the ambassador for the kingdom of heaven, God's mouthpiece, living and articulating the life of the kingdom. The pastor ministers the Word of God—and is ordained for such. In administering church life, pastors should be what they are supposed to be without modeling after a CEO guru using the secular styles or models in which the church is seen as a business with chains of command and bosses giving orders.

Techniques of administration alone do not make a successful leader. What a leader is as a person is of greater importance than the leadership role assumed. A Christian leader is first of all a Christian. With a God-directed life empowered by the Holy Spirit, Christian leaders must live what they profess. Their lives must be credible. They are God's men and women living out the life of Christ in the midst of His people. They are first and foremost a witness of God's grace. They serve not in order to benefit themselves, but that their congregants may know God, exhibit Christlikeness, and achieve spiritual maturity.[19]

"Be shepherds of God's flock that is under your care, serving as overseers—not because you must, but because you are willing, as God wants you to be; not greedy for money, but eager to serve; not lording it over those entrusted to you, but being examples to the flock" (1 Peter 5:2, 3, NIV).

---

1. Winton H. Beaven, "Ministerial Burnout—Cause and Prevention," *Ministry*, March 1986, 4, 5.

2. See Ellen G. White, *Patriarchs and Prophets* (Mountain View, CA: Pacific Press® Publishing Association, 1958), 301.

3. See White, *The Acts of the Apostles*, 92–94.

4. Ellen G. White, *Gospel Workers* (Washington, DC: Review and Herald® Publishing Association, 1915), 198.

5. Ellen G. White, *The Desire of Ages* (Mountain View, CA: Pacific Press® Publishing Association, 1898), 825; also read 818–828.

6. Ellen G. White, *Evangelism* (Washington, DC: Review and Herald® Publishing Association, 1948), 501.

7. Steven J. Lawson, "The Priority of Biblical Reading," *Bibliotheca Sacra,* April-June 2001, 198.

8. Eugene Peterson, *The Message: The New Testament in Contemporary English* (Colorado: NavPress, 1993), 2 Timothy 4:2–5.

9. White, *Christ's Object Lessons,* 128.

10. Ibid., 130, 131.

11. White, *Testimonies to Ministers and Gospel Workers,* 424.

12. White, *The Acts of the Apostles,* 209.

13. White, *Testimonies for the Church,* 7:18.

14. Russell Burrill, *Revolution in the Church* (Fallbrook, CA: Hart Research Center, 1993), 52.

15. White, *Christ's Object Lessons,* 365.

16. Os Guiness and John Seel, eds., *No God but God: Breaking With the Idols of Our Age* (Chicago: Moody Press, 1992), 124.

17. H. N. Malory, ed., *Wholeness and Holiness* (Grand Rapids, MI: Baker Book House, 1983), 240.

18. "Pointers," *The Ministry,* February 1968, 48.

19. R. D. Edwards, "Service Over Self-Interest," *Ministry,* November 1997, 29.

Chapter 9

The Pastor as a Community Leader

Steve D. Cassimy

Any pastor who wishes to have good influence in the church community needs to have significant relations with the external community that also result in effective pastoral operations. In a letter to me dated April 27, 2005, T. Wendell Foster, pastor and retired Bronx City Council member wrote the following, "The involvement of pastors in community can be traced back as far as the eighteenth century; then in 1793, one of the country's founding fathers, Benjamin Rush, called on pastors Richard Allen and Absalom Jones, to mobilize the black community during a yellow fever epidemic in Philadelphia."[1]

Foster, a favorite pastor in the South Bronx (a part of New York City), was elected to public office because of his community involvement. After a long and successful career as pastor/city councilman, Foster writes, "Today, for a pastor, it is essential that he/she becomes involved in community. If they are to fulfill the mandate of Jesus, 'Go ye into all the world . . .' they should become involved in the betterment of the community. They must go into schools, block associations, and community organizations to assist in organizing and empowering individuals to be productive. Being in a position of leadership, the pastor must be in touch with the community to keep his/her congregation informed, enlightened and empowered."[2]

My reference to the church community addresses the body of immediate believers who attend worship at a location within an external community. Many of these worshipers do not reside in the geographical area nor participate in the activities of the external community. They simply drive in to worship and at the end of the worshiping experience, they leave until the following week.

The external community consists of residents, institutions, and agencies, all of which are seeking ways to survive. They may include but are not limited to:

- The police precinct
- The hospitals
- The banks
- The political representatives
- Government agencies
- Private organizations
- Volunteer agencies

The problem

In the past history of pastoral education, we often took a hands-off attitude as far as the external community was concerned. The external community was seen as the state, and we were counseled as pastors never to involve the state in the life of the church. Statement after statement was read in reference to the joining of the church and state, so much so that grants, gifts, and other freebies were, to avoid misconceptions, refused. Ellen White says that, "Gospel ministers are to keep their office free from all things secular or political, employing all their time and talents in lines of Christian effort."[3] A statement like this has been used in times past to ignore involvement in community affairs. It is no secret that many of our ranks have compartmentalized society and the sacred. Thus, the church affairs were sacred, and all else was secular including the external community (according to this division). The pastor therefore remained free from community affairs because the only focus was to bring individuals into the fold of safety. Again, Ellen White declared to the General Conference of 1897 that "the saving of souls is to be our personal work, from which nothing is of sufficient moment to divert the mind."[4] These statements were taken literally and were not compared with other statements.

Another statement taken to mean the external community explains that "God calls upon them to enter their names as under His theocracy. He cannot approve of those who link up with worldlings. . . . Let us not forget that we are citizens of the kingdom of heaven. We are soldiers of the cross of Christ, and our work is to advance the interests of His kingdom."[5] On one hand, it seems therefore that Ellen White discouraged pastors from the community involvement. However, another picture emerges as one continues to carefully examine her counsel on community involvement.

A question in respect to receiving gifts and grants from "Gentiles and heathens" was posed to Mrs. White. Her answer is worth the quote. "The question is not strange; but I ask you who is it that owns our world? . . . Is it not God? He has an abundance in our world which He has placed in the hands of men by which the hungry might be supplied with food, the naked with clothing, the homeless with homes. . . . What they would give we should be privileged to receive."[6]

Ellen White considered that encouraging pastors to become acquainted with the community leaders in high places was important. She made reference to Joseph, the three faithful youth, Daniel, Nehemiah, and others who were directly involved in community. Her counsel to pastors today is powerful, "We should become acquainted with men in high places, and by exercising the wisdom of the serpent, and the harmlessness of the dove, we might obtain advantage from them, for God would move upon their minds to do many things in behalf of His people. . . .

"The Lord would have His people in the world, but not of the world. They should seek to bring the truth before men in high places, and give them a fair chance to receive and weigh evidence."[7]

With the church out of touch with the external community, it therefore cannot be considered a witness. Then, when the church tries to penetrate the external community once a year through its evangelistic efforts by saying that Jesus is the answer, few attend the meetings because they are asking one another, "What is the question?"

What can a pastor bring to the external community?

In his article "Finding our Place at the Table," John A. Lundblod suggests nine contributing factors that a pastor can bring to the community table:

1. A neighborhood presence.
2. The church's resource center.
3. The ability to convene gatherings.
4. The church as a sanctuary (a safe place).
5. A theological framework by which to understand life and events.
6. We can persist over a long time. Faith communities plan to stay for the "long haul" in a community. When other institutions abandon the community, the church remains.
7. We can bless and forgive. The pastor brings something far greater than any other agency to the table. The church can be a sacred place where people come for absolution, renewal, and new hope.
8. The pastors and their faith communities can provide spiritual support for the staff and volunteers of social service agencies.
9. Pastors and their faith communities can pray. The pastor can lift up community concerns in prayer, and the church community can pray for civic leaders and ask the guidance of the Spirit on community issues and efforts.[8]

Some may ask if a pastor has enough time to get involved with the external community, with so much to do in the church community. Lundblad points out that the pastor's place at the community's table can be compared to a deposit from which the pastor can make healthy withdrawals in the future. He sums it up this way: "There is no community issue—drug abuse, domestic violence, or juvenile delinquency—that cannot be found in one or more of the families at church. . . . Involvement by the pastor will bring the above contributions to the collaborative table; the pastor will also take back to the congregation knowledge skills and information valuable for members."[9] Community involvement is a tremendous investment that will yield great results in later years.

But as Lundblod eloquently suggests, "We are there to lift up in spiritual concerns and resources and to share what we have from our own community of believers."[10] Our presence testifies that God also works in the lives of the members of the community.

Training

Where does the Adventist pastor receive training to deal with the external community? Seventh-day Adventist colleges and seminary curriculum offer adequate guidance in areas of theology, religion, counseling, church administration, evangelism, and a host of other relevant pastoral-related fields but very little involvement with the community.

The conclusion over the years has been that we need to be more visible in our local communities. In the *Adventist Review* dated November 18, 2004, the General Conference president, Jan Paulsen, encouraged Adventists to be involved in the community. His remarks, slated for church members, pastors, and leaders, were made at an international conference on Adventists in the community. His message was direct and its significance could not be overlooked. He said that " 'We need a paradigm shift—service is service, and the focus should be on the people. After all, the church is part of the community, and we should help people feel that our presence in the community makes a difference to their welfare.' "[11]

This statement has lasting implications for the Adventist minister who needs to understand that as a pastor/shepherd, two constituencies are involved in community. First, there is what I choose to call the community of baptized members who are the inner circle of leadership for the community, since the church should serve the community. In addition, there is the wider constituency to whom the baptized membership must reach.

Pastors sometimes misunderstand this concept of community because many Adventist pastors view the church as a fortress. If indeed the church is a fortress, then in essence the pastor stands at the door to welcome the community, with the need for reaching out to the external community not a priority. Walt Kellenstad says it a little differently when he points out that as pastors, "Too often we have circled our wagons, created little enclaves of piety and worship, built walls around our communities of faith and invited people in only if they were willing to become like us."[12]

With our world becoming extremely secular, in this post-Christiandom, postmodern society, clearly the Adventist pastor needs to reconstruct the church's mission so that external community becomes aware of its presence and its influence. Historically, the Adventist pastor has been solely involved with the body of believers, and the primary role has been to care for their flock. This includes, but in no way limits, the caring for their spiritual, emotional, and physical needs. Definitely appropriate, for they will be held accountable; however, it cannot be considered the extent of the ministry, since the church exists to reach the external community. The pastor needs to understand the dual focus of the ministry—inward and outward.

Jesus and the external community

Replete with the encounters between Jesus and the external community recorded in the Gospels, the pastor/shepherd may conclude that Jesus spent more time with the external communities than with His church-membership community. Also important to observe in the Gospels is that Jesus seemed to be much more comfortable with the members of the community than those of the synagogue.

Jesus came to impact the whole world, not only His Jewish religious community, and that should serve as a springboard for the Adventist pastor. "Our faith and trust in God, our commitment to Jesus Christ, our belonging to the community of faith, the people of God, the church—all rest on the firm foundation of God's love for the world. The human community is the object: the city, the town, the neighborhood where we find ourselves."[13]

Sometimes, pastors are suspicious of the external community because outside of the safety of the church's walls evil prevails everywhere else. But from a quick glance of the Gospels, Jesus seemed much more comfortable in the presence of Mary Magdalene, Zacchaeus, and the woman caught in adultery than in the presence of the Scribes, Pharisees, the priests, and other church leaders.

Like Jesus, every pastor must impact the external community in some tangible way by involvement in and a commitment to community. The church's mission statement must reflect the church's intent to reach the community for Christ. John M. Buchanan was correct when he stated that "every church can do something to affirm and celebrate its community, the world around it, to say as eloquently and inaugauratively as possible that the human community is a wonder, that God loves the human community, that God's son came into it, demonstrating God's love to redeem and save it."[14]

As undershepherds, pastors must find traditional and/or creative ways to express that critical incarnational commitment to community. We are living in the closing moments of earth's history—the internal church must be in tune with the demands of the external community, so it can have an effective response. "Always, churches must live unapologetically and thoroughly in the world, in the midst of the human community where God calls us to be."[15]

Biblical evidence for pastoral involvement in community

From a brief look at the Gospels, listed here are several popular Bible characters with whom Jesus had significant interaction:

- The first miracle of Jesus at a community affair—John 2:1–11
- His involvement with the Samaritan woman—John 4:1–42
- The cleansing of a community outcast—Matthew 8:1–4
- The call of Matthew the tax collector—Matthew 9:9–12
- The woman caught in adultery—John 8:1–11
- The parable of the good Samaritan—Luke 10:25–37
- The supper at Simon's house—Matthew 26:6–13

In the Pauline writings, one of the most significant accounts of individuals involved in the community was a disciple named Tabitha (Dorcas).

She was not an apostle, or a pastor, but obviously from the account in Acts 9, she influenced and impacted her community in an astronomical way.

Conclusion

Involvement in the external community will reap substantial benefits for the pastor and the local congregation. The president of the General Conference placed the pastor's contribution to the external community in bold relief when he said that " 'We must make sure our mission is large enough to embrace Christ's care for suffering humanity. We are humanity; we are part of the world. This is where we live, this is where we work. God has placed us here for a purpose. We are expected by God to be instruments in His hands to reach into the community.' "[16]

Many pastors frequently ask: How can involvement in the external community enhance the Seventh-day Adventist pastor's ministry?

Some suggestions follow:

1. The pastor becomes visible in the community.
2. The pastor is perceived as one of the community's spiritual leaders.
3. The pastor becomes a friend of the community.
4. The pastor is perceived as credible.
5. The pastor can extend the church's facilities to the community when necessary.
6. The local church will qualify for available community resources.
7. The pastor will become acquainted with key community leaders.
8. The pastor will have access to key community players.
9. The pastor will have access to restricted areas in the community (e.g., the police precinct, the courthouse, parking privileges, job opportunities for members, etc.).
10. The pastor will be able to sit at the table where decisions that affect the church's community are made.

11. The pastor will be able to make a significant contribution, especially when important decisions are at stake.

12. The pastor becomes a liaison/bridge between the community and the local church.

13. The pastor has fewer barriers to break down as it relates to evangelism.

14. The pastor can significantly impact issues that relate to religious liberty.

15. The pastor is sought after for counsel.

16. The pastor develops respect in the community.

17. The church becomes a benefactor of the community's contacts and services.

18. The pastor will feel that he has made a positive contribution to the external community.

These suggestions are not to be considered complete, but can help us to orient ourselves in the multiple ways of possible involvement. My argument is that a pastor will not be as effective as he or she might be without community involvement.

---

1. T. Wendell Foster to the author, April 2, 2005.

2. Ibid.

3. Ellen G. White, *Testimonies for the Church,* 7:252.

4. Ellen G. White, *A Compilation: Spirit of Prophecy Counsels Relating to Church-State Relationships* (Silver Spring, MD: Ellen G. White Estate, 1964), 98.

5. Ibid., 113.

6. Ibid., 167.

7. Ibid.

8. John A. Lundblod, July–August 1999, "Lutheran Partners—Finding Our Place at the Table." Accessed February 23, 2005 from http://www.alca.org/lp/finding.html.

9. Ibid.

10. Ibid.

11. Jonathan Gallagher, "GC Promotes Adventists in the Community," *Adventist Review,* November 4, 2004, 18.

12. Walt Kallenstad, *Turn Your Church Inside Out: Building a Community for Others* (Minneapolis, MN: Augsburg Fortress, 2001), 10.

13. John M. Buchanan, *Being Church, Becoming Community* (Louisville, KY: Westminister John Knox Press, 1996), 5, 6.

14. Ibid., 22.

15. Ibid., 25.

16. Gallagher, "GC Promotes Adventists in the Community," 18.

Chapter 10

The Pastor as a Catalyst for Creating Special Ways to Enhance Special Services

James A. Cress

Your congregation needs some big deals—events that highlight the presence and ministry of your church.

This concept may offend some individuals who see no justification for the church to use marketing principles. Because some people equate marketing with manipulation, you even might find members who suspect any interaction with unchurched society beyond responding to direct inquiries from potentially interested individuals as scheming.

However, just because marketing strategies have sometimes employed questionable tactics or crass commercialization, the church should not unilaterally reject good opportunities to impact its surrounding society.

For example, the Gospels record times when Jesus utilized grand-scale events (big deals) that arrested mass attention. When Jesus fed five thousand, fellowshiped with foreigners, filled fishing boats until they sank, healed helpless cripples on the Sabbath, feasted with Pharisees, or overturned tables in the temple courtyard, He did not shy away from making a big deal out of an event that could have been conducted quietly. In fact, Jesus utilized the very public nature of these occasions to stimulate discussions about His activities and to focus attention on His central mission to seek and to save those who were lost.

Recently, I had the privilege of listening to the young pastoral team in Newfoundland, Canada, describe their conference-wide emphasis on raising awareness and increasing public participation in the activities of their congregations.

Since the church has long existed in Newfoundland's relatively isolated, island-bound society, you might wonder why heightening community awareness would receive priority. After all, logic would conclude that any long-time resident would be aware of the church's location and probably would know one of the members. However, these pastors are excited about the enhanced community interaction, cross-denominational fellowship, and increased attendance that has resulted from their intentional and strategic planning.

What are the "big deals" that they have conducted? Special days to honor police officers or fire fighters in their communities, interdenominational thanksgiving services, cultural events such as concerts and lectures, for example. Their enthusiastic description of their activities gave the following ideas practical life.

Every church can improve its image in the community. Churches in smaller communities can have greater impact on an established society by honoring others in the community who are known by all residents. Special events in larger, urban areas can attract newcomers who otherwise might not choose to attend any church function.

Advance planning is essential. To the extent that you want to include a broad base of community participation, coordinated scheduling and wide discussions provide buy-in. Remember, big deal events better emphasize joint, interactive participation more than a singular presentation by one group.

Excellence in production. Although available musical or speaking talent may widely vary from community to community, issues of precise timing, smooth transitions, strategic planning, and clear presentation conclusions impact excellence more than any individual superstar performer. Simple programming well executed is far better than complex presentations that stumble along for lack of rehearsal.

Capitalize on recurring opportunities. Most churches have child dedication services from time to time. What an opportunity to make certain that all relatives, friends, and coworkers of the parents receive invitations to attend and to participate as supporters for the youngster's special event. Prepare a nice program and follow up by mailing a copy of the dedication and sermon to each guest.

Remember the impact of spiritual events. Baptisms and Communion services are excellent times to invite the public to your services. Seventh-day Adventists practice open Communion, and that means that each individual believer, other than the church, makes the choice as to whether or not they participate. Also, baptisms bring conviction to those who witness the solemn event, who may begin their own preparations for discipleship as a result of observing someone else's immersion. It is helpful to note various options for examination of baptismal candidates or introduction of the elements of the Lord's Supper when guests attend.

Mark civic holidays. Special times such as Memorial or Remembrance Day, Veteran's Day, Mother's and Father's Day, and other holidays provide opportune moments to commemorate special segments of society and can easily be incorporated into your worship services. Likewise, religious seasons such as Advent or Easter may open the minds of the public to special services that your congregation can provide. In South America, for example, every Adventist church uses Easter week for special Holy Week evangelism programs.

Strategic goals are essential. Determine the purpose of your big deal event and stick to that focus. Do not attempt to sneak a different agenda into a program that has been advertised as a community event. Of course, you want to evangelize, but it is unfair to announce one thing and present another.

Results are more often long-term than immediate. Enhanced community appreciation for the church's role in society is a more likely goal of big deal events than immediately accessioning new members. However, remember that inactive members are often revitalized and unchurched individuals are often first recruited by public events.

Honor local heroes. Everyone enjoys seeing an individual honored for their contribution to local society. A plaque or gift book presented to a community leader makes a greater impact than importing a special guest from afar. Weeks after the event, people will recall and appreciate your congregation for having honored one of their own.

Advertising—a joint venture. If you're inviting the whole community, then solicit participation and sponsorship from local radio stations, newspapers, television channels, and community calendars to tell of the event. Advertise events that other churches are conducting and ask them to feature your events in their bulletins and announcements.

Appropriate follow-through. This includes providing opportunity for guests to register their attendance and be placed on a mailing list for future community events. However, do not presume that guests who register their attendance at your event are prepared for church recruitment, unless they specifically request additional information.

I encourage you to try some of these ideas for your own church and share your results with other leaders.

Chapter 11

The Pastor and the Little Things

D. Robert Kennedy

Pastoral leadership and the little things

Pastors lead with a visionary focus; they lead by peering into the future; they see not only far into the distance but also look at the big picture. Such capacity for visioning and dreaming incorporates one of the most important ingredients that will make for successful pastoral leadership. Without any attempt to argue the truth or falsehood of the views just presented, the truly successful pastor not only visions and dreams, but also has the capacity to focus on the little things—that is, be aware of the basics. Stated negatively, the argument suggests that many would-be successful pastors have failed, not because they have not been called of God, nor gifted by the Holy Spirit, nor understood their theology, nor skilled in their preaching, nor expansive in their vision, but they have failed in the little things. Pastoral attention to the little things demonstrates that a pastor can be a person of deep commitment, high competence, and extreme carefulness.

In this vein, Ellen White speaks of the qualities that make for successful Christian service when she says, "It is the duty of every Christian to acquire habits of order, thoroughness, and dispatch."[1] She further speaks of these qualities as those that show that a person has the capacity to maintain "high standards," "vigilance," and avoid "bungling at work of any character."[2]

The point is, as Malcolm Gladwell puts it, "little things can make a big difference." Gladwell uses several examples to make his point, such as showing how social epidemics work, how fashion trends develop, or how diseases become epidemics or pandemics, or how behavior patterns such as crime develop. He argues that what starts as little things then develops into big things. And further, that often what accounts for dramatic success is not what happens through the strategic plans, visions, goals, or rationalized timetable of a leader or organization, but the little things that tip the balance, moving from ordinary to extraordinary.[3]

Thus, while visionary leadership might focus on seeing the larger picture, leadership must also be made aware that the success of any visionary leadership consists of specific actions and particular reactions. Complex tasks are effectively completed only when one learns how to break down the complexity into simple steps. The things that often overwhelm our ministry might be made more accomplishable if we were to learn how to give greater attention to the little things about us. However, on balance, this emphasis should not lead us to think of micromanagement as a virtue, for micromanagers often miss the larger pictures that balance the little things. As Stephen Covey notes in his popular book on personal leadership, *7 Habits of Highly Effective People,* there are several little things that make for effectiveness in building one's emotional bank as a leader. Seven of which are presented in paraphrase form:

1. Being empathetic—attending to the hurts of others.
2. Being responsive—learning how to give feedback to keep open communication.
3. Being punctual—recognizing that it is the little minutes that make an hour and a day.
4. Being attentive—especially with children.
5. Being careful to keep commitments and promises.
6. Being aware of people—remembering to congratulate people's small efforts.
7. Being aware of protocols—many a public meeting gets destroyed because of the leader's lack of understanding regarding protocols.[4]

Covey's point emphasizes that a leader must see the big picture, but ought not to forget the little picture, for the little picture gives creative expression to the big picture.

My experiences as high school teacher and college and seminary professor have confirmed the popular notion that most of the students who make the top grades pay closest attention to the little things or task completion. They pay strict attention to their essay outlines, work with their grammatical constructions, and focus on editorializing the conflicts and contradictions that might be set forth within the first, second, third, or multiple drafts of their products. They read and reread sentences and paragraphs, thus finding ways to demonstrate commitment, competency, carefulness, efficiency, effectiveness, and other positive qualities that make for a well-rounded character.

Jesus and the little things

The one who best portrays giving attention to the little things without forgetting the larger picture was Jesus. He said it quite clearly, " 'He who is faithful in what is least is faithful also in much; and he who is unjust in what is least is unjust also in much' " (Luke 16:10, NKJV). While He sat in the temple in the worship service, He could have overlooked the widow who gave her mite, but He did not. His observation sought to challenge the ostentation of the Pharisees and build the faith of the disciples (Mark 12:43; Luke 21:2). When He was in a crowd and a woman touched His garment, He knew that virtue had left Him. The touch was a little thing, compared to the push of the crowd, and could have been left without public observation, but Jesus' comments drew the attention of the religious leaders, challenged their lack of compassion, and built the faith of the woman in a way that she received healing and forgiveness. She came to realize that her touch was not a contact with some magical spell but that she had been in contact with the Living God (Matthew 9:20, 21).

Jesus gave attention to the man in the sycamore tree. Although the crowd was very large, Jesus found time to look up to connect with one individual. Jesus asked him to come down so that He could share a meal with Him (Luke 19:4, 5). The list of examples as to how Jesus was exemplary in giving attention to the little things, little people, and little moments of life need not be extended. They are multiple, to say it mildly. Leighton Ford's point in his book, *Transformational Leadership,* was that Jesus understood that being connected to the role of the kingdom includes the ability to be faithful in the little things. He considered the little things significant if they were done to the honor and glory of God. On the contrary, the biggest accomplishment is too small if not done to the honor and glory of God.[5]

Little things that create an effective ministry

Effective ministry centers around giving attention to the little things that bring glory to the name of God—for instance, "scratching, where people are itching," giving some focus to where people are hurting, and "[catching up] the foxes . . . that spoil the vines" (Song of Solomon 2:15, NKJV).

In pastoral ministry, differences exist between giving serious attention to the little things and being distracted by trivialities—the little foxes that spoil the vines. Trivialities become distractive, diversionary, and even divisive. On the positive side, a list follows of little things that need serious attention:

1. Attending to the little things that lead to frustrations in communication. Pastoring coincides with relationship building. Relationships are either enhanced or destroyed by communication and break down when individuals are frustrated in communication. Pastors should take care to understand the utmost importance of frustrations that are created through the method or means of communication that they might choose to use. When frustrations occur, the wise pastor will seek to find ways of identifying the source of the frustration. Find ways of addressing it and reassure the person that the pastor will work hard to avoid such problems in the future. After a board meeting, for example, a pastor might have a brief meeting with a person who shows frustration, to ask for the source of the frustration, and if it shows authenticity, the pastor needs to share empathy and give the reassurance that better days are coming. It might be important to follow a stand-up meeting with a phone call, an e-mail, or a visit. With some of the little things that create frustrations in communication, it is important to note that:

- Pastors do not have to speak to every issue in the church.
- Pastors need to learn not to speak unless they have something to say.
- Pastors should be careful not to criticize the organization for which they work.
- Pastors need to practice returning phone calls. If a pastor cannot make a physical visit, make a phone call.
- Pastors need to remember that if they are going to be late for an appointment, they need to call ahead to make clear that they may not be able to meet the appointment when originally scheduled.

These little issues in communication are of great importance for effective pastoral practice.

2. Focusing on the appointment. Quite a few years ago, an incident struck so indelibly upon my mind that I am now quite careful when I agree to an appointment. A pastor invited me to preach in a certain church, but we did not communicate about the invitation for quite a few weeks. As the date drew near, I neglected to recheck with the pastor to confirm the appointment. On the day scheduled, I drove two hundred miles to the church, only to find that the pastor had invited another speaker for the same activity. The pastor and I spoke of the bungling. Was it my fault or the pastor's? I took the blame because I should have checked. Was I or the pastor at fault? You decide. My own negligence cost me a lot of gas, tire and body wear, and personal stress.

3. Attending to the little things that impact cross-cultural relationships. Having pastored in diverse cultures and taught in the area of cultural diversity, I am very convinced that attention to the little things can make a big difference in relationships with others. Any little thing that one does in a cross-cultural context that might make another person feel patronized can be very destructive. For example, one's facial expression, the distance one stands from another person, the tone of voice, and gestures are all little things that can make a big difference. Taking care before little things become big things becomes very important, especially in cross-cultural relationships.

4. Attending to the little things that impact those who are dealing with death and dying. This means learning what and when to speak and knowing the little things that will be helpful to the bereaved. Not every pastor will be a counselor but everyone needs to learn some of the little things that might be helpful to those among their flock who might be despairing. Remember the significance of a card sent after a funeral, a phone call, a short pastoral visit, or all three.

5. Attending to the little ones who are sometimes the invisibles of a community. Attention to the needs of the little tots, knowing their names, trying to find out their pain, and what makes them happy, are little things that make a big difference. As a pastor, I find that visiting the children's Sabbath Schools is very important because this gives me a great perspective on how their rooms are prepared and what their interactions are with those who teach them. I never take this part of my ministry for granted because through it, I can hear the imperative of Jesus to " 'Let the little children come to me, and do not hinder them, for the kingdom of heaven belongs to such as these' " (Matthew 19:14, NIV; Mark 10:14; Luke 18:16).

6. Attending to the little interests of the youth. Providing outlets for the youth can be listed as one of the most important little things in ministry. For example, much interest needs to be shared in what happens to the youth on Saturday nights. Not that the pastor needs to be the builder of activities for the youth on these nights, but they need to see to it that such small things happen. Delegate it, but hold responsible the person to whom you've delegated the task.

7. Attending to the little stresses of the middle-aged. The middle-aged can easily be taken for granted because they usually seem so healthy and secure. However, in reality, they are often anxious at this age because things begin to change. Many suffer deep frustrations and resentment because they may not have achieved their life's dream. They may thus become isolated and need to be reminded that their lives have bigger goals than the mere transient. They do desire even a little attention, especially as they face the radical transformations that will lead them into their next stage of life. In this case, pastors needs to ask themselves what can be done to enhance the lives of this age group.

8. Attending to the elderly, especially the sick and shut-ins. The noted writer Maurice Roberts states in one of his collected articles in *Great God of Wonder* that "in a church climate where concern for 'youth' is always kept at fever-pitch, it is understandable that many of the best and most faithful members feel like second-class citizens because they are now elderly, and overlooked." Roberts also states that this aspect of ministry might be considered "simple." However, he encourages ministers to know they would be sinning against Christ if they neglect the souls of the elderly believers who look to them for some words of occasional encouragement and receive none. He insists that this is a ministry that no Christian ought to shun.[6]

9. Attending to the little dirt and rubbish in the physical plant of the church. Is this the pastor's business too? Most of the churches I have been called to pastor needed repairs and renovation. I've wondered, *Is this a special calling from God?* Sometimes I go to the church with big goals—all I am going to do in this church is preach and train lay members to do witnessing. However, I have found it hard to be an effective pastor in a dirty building so, within each pastorate and during the first year, I am in a repair or renovation program. Revival, reformation, and church growth are always more effectively carried out with a clean building. While the cleanliness of a church might not have as much to do with the mission of the church as the delivery of a good sermon, yet the cleanliness of the church sets a better context for a great sermon.

10. Attending to the little things that impact the church's visibility in the community. When I served as a vice president for Enrollment Management at Atlantic Union College, my staff used to state in our debriefing meetings that "image is everything." The concept, taken from the marketing industry, was used to evaluate the particular context in which it was said, but is also true in any context where one tries to make an impact. The kind of sign that one has at a church, the kind of lighting, and other little physical things that impact the image of the church should not be passed over lightly, for when not properly in place, they make a negative statement.

11. Attending to the little things that cause stress and burnout. Sometimes we as pastors give too much credence to the little comments that are made about us, so much so that we suffer stress and burnout. Noted more for younger pastors rather than older ones, but as a pastor gets older, they find that losing a night's sleep over pettiness can be so debilitating that they often decide that it is not worth it. However, younger pastors can become destroyed by turning the little molehills into mountains. Although the reference centers on the impact of little things on younger pastors, pastors should never get the impression that older colleagues are immune. Because of personality, it might be that some pastors never learn how to let go of these little, negative things. So to everyone in ministry, never forget that we are instructed to cast all our cares upon Him, for He cares for us (1 Peter 5:7).

12. Attending to the little networks in the communities we lead. Many pastors have become quite frustrated because their visions for their congregations have been bogged down in elders' meetings or church boards or in other boards or committees. An analysis of a congregation reveals that some pastoral leaders do not know how to use a congregation's communication network. Stated negatively, whether we like it or not, we have to admit that in congregations certain clicks, personalities, and channels impact communication. We can either disdain these groups and not have much accomplished or we can recognize them, learn how to use or bypass them, and get our work completed. If pastors would observe the little networks in their congregations and know how to mediate them, they might alleviate a lot of stress.

13. Attending to our posture, whether we are or are not sitting upfront. I was vividly reminded of this while writing this chapter, because a few friends were observing me at a certain meeting we attended. I was sitting in the middle of the audience with one hand over my eyes during a certain presentation, and some friends felt that I was responding negatively. Really, I did feel a little frustrated at the presenter because of my feeling of the disjunction between presentation and practice. I did try to sit quietly and respectfully with my hand resting on my desk and my face slightly covered, with what I thought was neutral expressions, but my friends, who were supposedly conscious of my analysis of the situation, came to me later and said, "We were looking at you for an expression, and did not see one, but your hand over your eyes said something." Our postures can definitely impact a congregation. Yes, 70 percent or more of our communication is body language. The point here is that people take a lead from the leader, so we must lead positively with presence and posture.

14. Attending to how we say Yes and No. Someone gave me a little sign that I used to keep behind my door (it could be a turn-off for some people) when I taught college. It reads, "I can only serve one person a day. Sorry today is not your day and tomorrow does not look good either." It sounds harsh, doesn't it? Not many students noticed it. However, every time I looked at the sign, it said something about the need to be careful about the two little words *Yes* and *No* (cf. Matthew 5:37). How do we say them? We need to learn appropriateness and discipline in the little answers we give to people because they do have a great impact on our credibility in the broadest areas of leadership. For example, saying Yes to everyone will create confusion in our scheduling, and saying No at all times will make us seem to be the meanest of persons. The point is that we ought to create balance with our *yeses* and *nos*.

Some positive consequences of minding the little things

Since there are negative consequences when one fails to attend to the little things and positive consequences when one attends to them, let us find the best path to more healthy practices by getting our pastoral priorities in place. Here are some stated consequences as reminders of the benefits of reaction to the little things:

1. Faithfulness in little things points to our integrity. Integrity is the character ingredient that builds trust in any leadership. Faithfulness in little things (that is habits, abilities, and attitudes) builds our character. In the long run, it is our character that counts. Leadership specialists count it as an axiom that the "greatest crisis of leadership today is a crisis of character." Or we might say like Peter Drucker, "quality of character doesn't make a leader, but lack of it flaws the entire process."[7]

2. Faithfulness in little things demonstrates our competence and effectiveness. On the issues of competence and effectiveness, we can note, for example, that it is the little adjustments that we make in organizational strategies that keep chaos or a constancy of "perpetual organizing."[8] The day-to-day efforts keep the organization oiled so that the whole system will not wear or tear.

3. Faithfulness in little things builds our relationships with others. People are not so concerned about what you say as they are about who you are when you are with them. When members ask for letters to commend them or to secure their faith in their jobs or school situations, the pastor needs to provide those documents.

4. Faithfulness in little things keeps us away from crisis management. When we avoid the little things that are to be done day by day, we enter into those moments of pressure because we now have more to do than we can get done.

5. Faithfulness in little things ultimately helps us to overcome stress. Excessive stress can be dangerous for our health, mentality, and spirituality.

6. Faithfulness in little things is often the commendation that we receive for greater responsibilities. " 'His master replied, "Well done, good and faithful servant! You have been faithful with a few things; I will put you in charge of many things. Come and share your master's happiness!" ' " (Matthew 25:21, 23, NIV).

Quite a few ministers do spend an exorbitant amount of time, energy, and finances on the tangible aspects of their ministry. But some of the same minimize the little things that would create the balance that they need for success. Although some things in ministry need to have great priority, all aspects of ministry must be attended to for success.

As a lad, a sermon that impacted me most was one preached by a now-retired minister, Pastor Zadock Reid, who lives in California. He titled the sermon "One Little Thing." Then he used multiple examples to make his point. He spoke of a great redwood tree in California that had fallen because of rot at its core. Little creatures had eaten into its top root and into its heart, and one day it became so weak that it toppled. He also spoke of a little cigarette butt that was thrown at the edge of a forest and consequently burned thousands of acres. He mentioned the little stick of match used to create a fire, then he made an appeal that we must stop taking little sins for granted. I can still hear his shrill voice that had a profound impact on me to give greater attention to the little things.

Today we might ask, "How might our legacy of ministry be the blessing God intended it to be?" I would answer, "Give some attention to the little things that impact effectiveness and competence." Like the little song we sang in Sabbath School when we were little, "Brighten the corner where you are. Brighten the corner where you are. Someone far from harbor you may guide across the bar. Brighten the corner where you are." One tragedy of ministry is that sometimes there are those who want to change the world church, while they cannot even pastor the little flock they have been given to attend.

Activities

1. Think of three little things that might have threatened your ministry and remind yourself of how you dealt with them so that today you have a more positive ministry.

2. Think of three little things that have enhanced your ministry, and that you might recommend to a ministerial colleague suffering frustrations.

3. Think of three little things to which you wish to attend that you believe if dealt with might give your ministry a more positive impact today.

---

1. Ellen G. White, *Christian Service* (Hagerstown, MD: Review and Herald® Publishing Association, 1947), 237. The statements of "Qualifications for Successful Christian Service" on pages 223–256 are followed by statements framed under the rubric "Assurance of Success."

2. Ibid.

3. Malcolm Gladwell, *The Tipping Point: How Little Things Can Make a Big Difference* (New York: Little, Brown and Company, 2000, 2003), 15–29.

4. Steven Covey, *7 Habits of Highly Effective People: Restoring the Character Ethic* (New York: Simon & Schuster, 1989), 236–260.

5. Leighton Ford, *Transforming Leadership: Jesus' Way of Creating Vision, Shaping Values & Empowering Change* (Downers Grove, IL: InterVarsity Press, 1991), 97, 98. In a whole chapter of his work, Dr. Ford, focused on the character of those leaders who are kingdom builders, by noting that they need to give greater attention to little things.

6. Maurice Roberts, *Great God of Wonders* (Edinburgh: The Banner of Truth Trust, 2003), 95.

7. Quoted in *The Christian Educator's Handbook on Teaching*, K. O. Gangel and H. G. Hendricks, eds. (Grand Rapids, MI: Baker Book House, 1988), 245.

8. Charles A. Tidwell, *Church Administration: Effective Leadership for Ministry* (Nashville, TN: Broadman & Holman Publishers, 1985), 207.

Chapter 12

Interns and Mentors

Walton A. Williams

Ellen White's strong position and frustration regarding the training of young pastors appeared twice in 1890 when she wrote: "The importance of these things has been shown me so many times that I feel a burden on this point;" and, "I think this has been shown me twenty times in my lifetime, and I have tried to tell it to the brethren, but the evil is not remedied."[1] This chapter considers what she advocated and how to put it in twenty-first-century ministry context.

Ministry formation in Adventist history began as early as 1870 when James White launched the Ministers Lecture Association of Seventh-day Adventists, where for five dollars a year (women Bible workers could join for three dollars), pastors could attend a series of Bible lectures and receive grammar and penmanship instruction. In 1881, a General Conference committee known as the Committee on Course of Reading for Ministers established a six-year required reading plan where license committees in each conference were to annually insure that this reading was completed by employees (amusingly and not surprisingly, the program only lasted four years).

Concern in this area continued when in 1919, A. G. Daniells, then General Conference president, challenged the "teachers (of pastors) to really change or greatly improve the class of preachers among us."[2] Increasingly, Adventist leadership considered plans that would stimulate interest in, coordinate selection for, and train young men and women in pastoral work.

Finally, during the April 1929 Annual Council meeting, Adventist leaders formalized an inclusive method of training pastors entitled, "A Ministerial Internship Plan." Financial assistance was made available for this new "field training" under the supervision of an experienced worker.[3] Interest in this new plan led J. L. McElhany, new General Conference president, to write in the *Review and Herald:* "of all the questions considered by the Council, this one proved the most interesting."[4]

In light of the previous practice of placing young, inexperienced men directly over churches, often with disastrous results,[5] Daniells quoted numerous conference presidents who heartily affirmed the plan. By September of that year, the program's success (sixty young men and women placed) fueled an "enthusiastic assent" to its perpetuity,[6] thus birthing the Adventist ministerial internship program.

The Adventist internship model was based on the latest modality in adult education-supervision. Arising from the American Industrial Revolution, supervision[7] concentrated on tasks to be mastered. For ministerial interns, this included specific pastoral tasks/skills considered critical to pastoral success. From the first list of eight such tasks mentioned in 1919 by A. G. Daniells,[8] the list grew to twenty-four by 1926,[9] and to fifty by 1990.[10]

Over the last century, an increasing emphasis has been placed on the academic preparation of Adventist pastors. Schools for ministry formation have spread feverishly wherever the message of Christ's return has been preached, until now there are some one hundred colleges, seminaries, and universities around the globe preparing these men and women.[11] Adventism can boast that its ministers are the best academically prepared pastors in the world.[12]

So what is wrong with this picture? Surely after one hundred-plus years and such educational muscle, we have met Ellen White's recommendation for ministry preparation! But sadly, the limitations of such formal pastoral education are becoming apparent. Administrators, members, and authors now realize that a balance between intellectual concepts and what happens in real congregational life cannot be developed in formal classroom settings alone. Indeed, "practical contact with the changing world . . . is . . . essential to education in theological thinking."[13]

Case in point: Al graduated from a fine Adventist theology undergraduate program. Hired by a conference, his internship started abruptly by being instructed to visit all the missing young members and encouraging them to reengage with the local congregation. Not only did he not have any idea of how to make a pastoral visit, but he had never chaired a board, baptized or anointed anyone, held an evangelistic series, or personally done any of the usual ministerial functions. He learned each of these skills as the need arose, often with disastrous, embarrassing, or humorous results.

An interesting research prepared for the dean of the Seventh-day Adventist Theological Seminary at Andrews University in 1982 evaluated the post-seminary field education its graduates experienced. Not surprisingly, 124 seminarians said their greatest need was for someone "who would spend more time with them modeling and training in all aspects of pastoral ministry," and 89 of the responding supervisors desired "more opportunity for supervision, modeling and reflection on progress." Ellen White would have been disappointed again as the research concluded, "in general, pastors did not do a great deal of showing interns how to successfully perform certain tasks vital to the ministry."[14]

Across the world divisions, beginning Adventist pastors continually are sent directly into the field to evangelize, oversee, and grow healthy churches with little to no prior pastoral experience. To assist and bridge such lapses, the General Conference Ministerial Association, in 1990, prepared a *Manual for Seventh-day Adventist Ministerial Interns and Intern Supervisors.*[15] This 116-page manual, intended to regularize and improve the internship experience for Adventist interns, exposed and evaluated them on fifty ministerial skills/functions. Unfortunately, use of the *Manual* often became either task-oriented, superficial, or nonexistent. Consequently, few senior pastors or interns utilize this equipping handbook or have substituted a satisfactory alternative.[16]

Inasmuch as a replacement has become necessary, the climate is ideal for implementing a new intern training attitude and tactic.[17] Perhaps now we should be serious about the recommendation of Ellen G. White 117 years ago. What specifically did she say and how can we accomplish it?

On July 14, 1890, E. G. White gave a talk to the General Conference Committee as they met at Lake Goguac just outside Battle Creek, Michigan. She expressed concern about overworked and aging workers[18] in fields of labor. In this same context, she expressed frustration about competent and promising young workers, who could be a blessing but "should not be sent out alone. They should stand right by the side of older and experienced ministers, where they could educate them. . . .

"I think this has been shown me twenty times in my lifetime, and I have tried to tell it to the brethren; but the evil is not remedied."[19]

Whether by design or of necessity, our spiritual forefathers frequently thrust aspiring young pastors into the realities of pastoral ministry by the "sink or swim" method. Amazingly, some were a success while others were overwhelmed and perhaps unnecessarily sank. While the unusually gifted somehow find a way to succeed, many lesser-talented men are thrown into substantial ·ministry leadership positions with nigh little ministry formation.[20]

It was Ellen White's repeated desire that preparation for Adventist pastoral ministry would utilize some form of mentorship. Her statements regarding the advisability of placing younger men alongside older, more experienced men undoubtedly influenced the final adoption in 1929 of the Ministerial Internship Plan.[21] This also underscores why, in 1932, the intern plan was further structured so that field exposure would be accomplished under qualified supervision[22] and why the 1990 *Manual for Seventh-day Adventist Ministerial Interns and Intern Supervisors* would promote supervision as *the* method of ministry formation.

Some questions loom on the horizon to be answered. Is our current ministry preparation practice really developing the best agents to finish the Lord's work? Does our apocalyptic haste to just send in more replacements have a dark side? Are we in fact veering from inspired counsel in order to get spiritual "producers" out to the field so the organization can see a goodly return on its educational investment?

The recent explosion of adult learning literature may reflect Adventism's need to reconsider its *modus operandi* for ministry formation. An overview of recent mentoring/coaching literature reveals specific advantages organizations experience that utilize such relationships for entry level employees. Interestingly, most people can mentor provided they are willing to share what they have learned[23] because, at its core, mentoring/coaching describes adults who transfer experience and expertise to someone less equipped.

The differences between mentoring and coaching can be described as: coaching relates primarily to performance improvement in a specific skill area, whereas mentoring relates primarily to the identification and nurturing of the whole person's potential—life maturation. Another way to express this is that counseling mainly deals with the past, mentoring deals with the present, and coaching works toward our future.

This leaves us with three searing questions regarding ministry formation:

1. What is the purpose of ministerial internship?
2. What core characteristics do good mentors/coaches have?
3. If mentoring and/or coaching are a superior method over supervision in ministry formation, what would it look like should this be adopted for training ministers for Seventh-day Adventist organizations on a worldwide scale?

First: What is the purpose of a ministerial internship?

The ministerial internship period balances the tension between academic and practical ministerial training, without which Adventist interns easily fall into one or the other extremes. From inception, ministry internship was to be a time of practical training under the leadership of experienced pastors and evangelists.[24] To affirm this, the General Conference Ministerial Association published a helpful internship guideline in 1968 entitled, *So You're an Intern: Guidelines for Ministerial Interns.*

Rolf H. Kvinge,[25] in an excellent dissertation on this topic, maintains that the purpose of the internship period is to:

1. be trained into the ministerial profession by a minister-supervisor;
2. learn how to apply biblical truth in real-life situations;
3. prove one's call to ministry;
4. experience providing administration for a church;
5. learn to win people to Jesus; and
6. do personal witnessing for Christ and teach lay members to do likewise.

While the specific time allotted for ministerial internship may vary from one organization to another, its purpose remains clear. Adventist publications consistently sound the same message: a ministerial internship is a period for practical ministry training served under the guidance of a qualified minister to introduce one to ministry life and to verify their call to ministry,[26] a time when the intern "is expected to learn, to observe and to serve," a specified time to "learn as much about the practical operation of all departments of the church and soul-winning as possible,"[27] and to "actualize the seminary knowledge in the living situation of the church."[28]

In an undated publication by E. G. White and A. O. Olsen, the following necessary qualifications are listed as important ministry preparation:[29] (1) a thorough understanding of the truth, (2) a practical experience in saving grace, (3) a general personal conversion from self and sin, (4) an intimate knowledge of Christ, and (5) a daily experience in the things of God.[30] How will the employer adequately establish that such has occurred, or can be adequately determined through the normal verbal examination by an ordination examination committee?[31]

But ministerial internship includes more than the development of skills; ministry formation is about the development of the whole person. Authenticity of character is of higher importance in spiritual ministry than expertise. Internship should be as fully about the kind of people we build for service as it is about how many souls they have or can baptize. Ministry is about *being* as well as *doing;* about shaping the heart that far surpasses the honing of skills. And these qualities do not happen in isolation.

Second: What core characteristics do good mentors/coaches have?

Mentoring is not all that hard to accomplish! You do not need to read numerous books on the subject nor master the intricacies of mentoring/coaching, though that would be admirable. Mentoring is simply an experienced person pouring themselves into an apprentice until the latter has achieved an expected level of expertise and can in turn mentor someone else to spiritual maturity.

Ellen G. White beautifully addressed the mentor's limitation and privilege when she wrote, "It is not possible to advise in every particular the part that the youth should act; but they should be faithfully instructed by the older workers, and taught to look ever to Him who is the author and finisher of our faith."[32]

Brian Dudar, who may have been the first *Ministry* magazine author to express an intern's need for a mentor,[33] may not have realized it at the time, but he touched all the best characteristics of a good mentor. He wished for a mentor who was wise, had an honest self-disclosure, was transparent, would be a friend, was competent, would share challenging church responsibility, would be an inspiring evaluator, was one who fostered individuality, and able to set the mentee free.[34]

How does an intern find such a mentor? The first characteristic to look for is their ability to relate with you. While mentorships concentrate on the intern's growth, the journey should be enjoyable—therefore, you need someone to whom you can relate and enjoy being with. Look for someone who will help as well as allow you to grow (not the personification of all knowledge).

Ask them if they would mentor you for the next six to twelve months, or longer if both of you choose to do so. Meet no less than once a month, plus be in some form of contact every two weeks. As an intern, be responsible for what you want to learn and faithful to all commitments regarding the mentor relationship. Watch each other perform under various situations and dialogue and debrief afterward regarding what was experienced, assumed, missed, or needs improving.

Probe together the theological insights and reflections possible in each situation while looking for the hand of God behind and around all events.

Challenge and be challenged to think deeper and clearer about spiritual insights and potentials. Be open about shortcomings and vulnerable to offers of help. Learn from your mentor's assets and liabilities as to how God can work with the weakest of the weak.

A mentor's value to an intern will come from the three core character traits that Peter Wilson's research found all exemplar mentors to have: "The mentor relationship is one of the most complex and developmentally important a [person] can have in early adulthood. . . . No word currently in use is adequate to convey the nature of the relationship we have in mind here. . . . Mentoring is defined not in terms of formal roles but in terms of the character of the relationship and functions it serves."[35]

1. Integrity. All relationships, especially those between mentors and interns, hinge on a sense of trust. Trust becomes impossible when integrity is absent from one's character, with trust as the fabric that makes relationships possible. Trust can be described as a state of confidence and comfort in relation to another person. Ideal mentoring relationships are characterized by honesty, some degree of self-disclosure, and mutuality.

2. Courage. Mentoring frequently requires courageous thought and action on the part of the mentor. Also, interns tend to copy the courage of their mentors when facing the anxiety the new challenges and the unfamiliar demands of ministry. While mentors must be courageous enough to know and manage themselves, they demonstrate courage in their own optimistic view of the future. With ministry often made manageable through a "courage-by-proxy process," such courage, exhibited by mentors, insures that an intern's performance will be enhanced and significant errors likely decreased.

3. Care. Caring mentors value the distinct personhood of their interns, devote considerable time to hearing and understanding them, work to discern their specific talents and vulnerabilities, provide an affirmation-rich environment for them to experiment with new identities, and weather the tribulations that accompany crisis and growth. Caring mentors clearly communicate their value of the intern and consistently work to further their best interests and ultimate goals.[36]

Third: If mentorship and/or coaching is a superior method over supervision in ministry formation, what would it look like for Seventh-day Adventist organizations on a worldwide scale?

The explosive growth of the Adventist Church requires methodologies translatable across continents and cultures in the preparation of ministry candidates. The beauty of Ellen White's up-to-date inspired counsel includes being transportable for our world church. Mentoring and/or coaching works, no matter what country or culture context. Mentoring ministerial interns also becomes cost-effective. It does not require retraining or added staff—just a one-to-one commitment between an experienced and inexperienced minister to journey together for the professional grounding of the latter. Neither does mentoring require immediate proximity or multiple staff relationships. Mentoring is about access rather than location, about availability, experience, willingness, and perspective.

Expediting mentoring on a worldwide scale is as simple as a personal or organizational commitment that no ministerial intern will begin ministry alone. This commitment would include the employer promoting an intentional paring between an intern and an experienced coworker of the intern's choice.[37] For a predetermined period of time,[38] each intern enters this "finishing school" of ministry preparation, experiencing all aspects of actual ministry under the supportive care and counsel of one totally committed, authentic mentor. How would it work?

Employers:

- Encourage/insist all interns to choose a mentor/coach for a stated period of time (six to twenty-four months).
- Facilitate (where possible) intern/mentor meetings.
- Reward mentor's investment of time.
- Use mentor's input regarding ordination readiness.
- Expect mentorship to be replicated after internship.

Mentors:

• Are available to intern's ministry growth needs.
• Meet with interns on predetermined regular intervals.
• Ask more questions and give less answers to encourage self-discovery.
• Listen more than talk.
• Offer and expect balanced and reflective feedback.
• Be transparent and authentic.
• Celebrate termination of mentorship.

Interns:

• Are responsible for keeping all appointments and setting agenda of need.
• Expect more questions than answers.
• Are prepared to think thoroughly and relationally.
• Strive to be honest about areas of weakness.
• Follow through on all expectations and suggestions.
• Negotiate and communicate with mentor.
• Honor mentor's investment in them.
• Expect mentorship termination

Who knows, perhaps this model of ministry formation was what Ellen White envisioned. It's surely worth trying![39]

---

1. Ellen G. White, *Manuscript* 19b, 1890, in *Evangelism* (Washington, DC: Review and Herald® Publishing Association, 1946), 684.

2. Official Minutes of August 1, 1919, Seventh-day Adventist Bible Conference, 1256.

3. Provision was made for up to one hundred students, fifteen of whom were to be female Bible workers. Further evidence for female inclusiveness is found in the 1932 Autumn Council minutes: "Young men and women in our training schools desiring to make application for ministerial internship shall fill out completely the application blanks provided."

4. *The Advent Review and Sabbath Herald,* June 9, 1929. Also very positive review by Joseph M. Ramsey, ed., "Reviews," *The Expositor* (Cleveland, OH: F. M. Barton Co.,

1929), 1178. For a further report by A. G. Daniells, see the July 1929 inaugural issues of *Ministry* magazine.

5. Ibid. Minutes indicate much concern voiced over the lack of field education. For example, E. K. Slade, president of Atlantic Union, responded from the floor of the GC Council: "There is no branch of our organized work (pastoral implied) where there is more uncertainty. . . . Our present policy is to place inexperienced men in charge of districts, making them pastor of churches, or perhaps we might call them president of little conferences placing them in these positions right from the start. Consequently, these young men are coming up against problems which they are not prepared to handle."

6. General Conference Committee Official Minutes of April 30, 1929. As the primary design was to service candidates under the age of thirty, exception was made for those who "in later life have had to postpone the advantages of a Christian education, and who may be accepted up to thirty-five years of age."

7. "Supervision means the act of watching over the work or tasks of another who may lack full knowledge of the concept at hand. Supervision does not mean control of another but guidance in a work, professional or personal context." From http://en .wikipedia.org/wiki/Supervision. Accessed June 9, 2009.

8. Ibid., 1919. These include: (1) honesty, sincerity, true to their consciences; (2) the importance of studiousness; (3) regularity in their habits of studying, working, and living; (4) the importance of Bible study and constancy with the Bible; (5) the appearance, the manners, and the deportment of the minister; (6) the use of chaste, select language; (7) methods in public—his conduct; and (8) pulpit manners.

9. Ibid., General Conference Autumn Council Minutes of 1926.

10. *Manual for Seventh-day Adventist Ministerial Interns and Intern Supervisors* (Washington, DC: General Conference Ministerial Association, 1990).

11. Based on the *Seventh-day Adventist Yearbook 2007* (Hagerstown, MD: Review and Herald Publishing Association, 2007).

12. It is exceedingly rare that any denomination requires both undergraduate and graduate level education for its pastors, as the Seventh-day Adventist Church does, as is spelled out in the church's working policy.

13. David S. Schuller, "Part I: Theological Education at Level II," *Theological Education* (Spring 1968): 675, 676.

14. Roger L. Dudley, Kim White, and Des Cummings Jr., *A Study of the Ministerial Internship as Perceived by Seminary Students and their Former Supervisors:* a report prepared for the office of the Dean of the Seventh-day Adventist Seminary, May 1882. The report concluded "that the major weakness of the internship program is the lack of experiences in which the supervisory pastor models ministerial behaviors for the intern and in which the pastor observes and critiques ministerial behaviors performed by the interns" (p. 19). A contrary opinion can be found in Earlington Winston Guiste's "An Assessment of Practicing SDA Ministers' Perceived Administrative Skills: Implications for Curriculum in Ministerial Training" (PhD thesis, Michigan State University, Ann Arbor, Michigan, n.d.). "SDA ministers are not academically prepared to adequately

assume the administrative responsibilities of the local churches, and they are victims of the church's educational system" (p. 2).

15. *Manual for Seventh-day Adventist Ministerial Interns and Intern Supervisors* (Washington, DC: General Conference Ministerial Association, 1990).

16. Worthy exceptions and adaptations occurred in some conferences and unions. See David VanDenburgh, "The Intern Supervisor Training Event," *Ministry,* October 1995, 20. The author advocates a certified training course focusing on developing persons rather than skills and promoting relationships between intern and supervisor. The training combines mentoring, spiritual friendship, and teaching via the use of critical incident.

17. At the time this chapter is being written, a revised edition is being completed.

18. In 1929, a report stated that "The provision is designed to fill the depleted ranks of workers in the North American conferences, many of which have given to the point of exhaustion to our world mission fields" (*The Ministry,* July 1929, 6).

19. Ellen G. White, *Manuscript* 19b, 1890, as quoted in *Sermons and Talks,* vol. 2 (Silver Spring, MD: Ellen G. White Estate, 1994), 81, 82.

20. See endnote 5.

21. "In gaining a preparation for the ministry, young men should be associated with older ministers. Those who have gained an experience in active service are to take young, inexperienced workers with them into the harvest-field, teaching them how to labor successfully for the conversion of souls" (*Gospel Workers,* 101). "It is God's desire that those who have gained an experience in His cause, shall train young men for His service" (Ibid.,102). "Brethren of experience . . . should feel a responsibility upon them to take charge of these young preachers, to instruct, advise, and lead them, to have a fatherly care for them" (*Testimonies for the Church,* 1:443).

22. For an excellent Adventist historical perspective of ministerial training, as well as an educational philosophy in ministerial education, see Rolf H. Kvinge's "A Proposed Training Program for Seventh-day Adventist Ministerial Interns in the Scandinavian Countries" (DMin dissertation, James White Library, Andrews University, 1982).

23. According to Tim Elmore, "we simply cannot do mentoring well if we don't do relationships well" (*Mentoring, How to Invest Your Life in Others* [Indianapolis, IN: Wesleyan Pub. House, 1995], 45).

24. John F. Neufeld and others, eds., *Seventh-day Adventist Encyclopedia* (Washington, DC: Review and Herald® Publishing Association, 1976), 900, s.v. "Minister."

25. Rolf H. Kvinge, "A Proposed Training Program for Seventh-day Adventist Ministerial Interns in the Scandinavian Countries" (DMin dissertation, Andrews University, 1982).

26. *Ministerial Internship Guide,* a document on file at the Center for Adventist Research (DF 97-i-1), 1, at Andrews University. " 'Ministerial Internship' as here used includes the fifth and sixth years of theological training and a one-year period of service spent in practical training in ministerial labor or Bible instructor's work, to be entered upon after the completion of the preparatory theological course or its equivalent. This field training period is served under supervision in a local conference, at a limited wage,

for the purpose of proving the divine call to the ministry or to the Bible instructor's work."

27. Ibid., 2, 4. See also Kvinge's dissertation on a summary of Adventist expectations for ministerial training and internship.

28. *So You're an Intern: Guidelines for Ministerial Interns* (Silver Spring, MD: General Conference Ministerial Association, 1958), 2, 3.

29. Ellen G. White and O. A. Olsen, "Appeal and Suggestions to Conference Officers in Regard to the Development and Elevation of the Gospel Ministry," Center for Adventist Research, Andrews University.

30. Ibid.

31. "The General Conference wisely refrained from stating any definite scheme for the inflexible guidance of examining committees" (Ibid., 9).

32. Ellen G. White, *Gospel Workers*, 102.

33. See "Expectations of an Intern Pastor," *Ministry*, March 1994, 24.

34. See also document DF97-i-1, *An Action Voted by the Seventh-day Adventist North American Committee on Administration* that recognized that "the new graduate very much needs wise and sympathetic counsel in the period in which he adjusts from formal schooling to the activities and problems of the local church and to field evangelism."

35. Peter F. Wilson, "Core Virtues for the Practice of Mentoring," *Journal of Psychology and Theology*, Summer 2001, vol. 29, no. 2. These three are founded on the author's synopsis of Paul's list in 1 Corinthians 13:13.

36. Adapted from Wilson.

37. All mentoring literature strongly advocates the advantage of paring choice being by the mentee rather than the organization or mentor. Such initiative by the mentee cements the trust factor, thus making growth more from the incentive of the mentee than the mentor.

38. Clear expectations for the health of the relationship demand time frames.

39. A worthwhile ministry mentorship resource is Randy D. Reese and Keith R. Anderson, *Spiritual Mentoring: A Guide for Seeking and Giving Direction* (Downers Grove, IL: InterVarsity Press, May 1999).

Chapter 13

Leadership Matters: Cultural Competence for Ministerial Leaders

Leslie N. Pollard

Cultural expert Geert Hofstede observed, "Like many human characteristics, leadership is in the eye of the beholder—in particular, of those led. Just as the consumer and not the producer is the proper judge of the quality of a produce, so it is the followers and not the leaders themselves who know best about the quality and effectiveness of leadership."[1]

I agree with Hofstede in the foregoing assertion. For too long, ministerial leaders have tended to define leadership effectiveness from our internal points of reference only. These points have included time spent in visitation, soul winning, fund-raising, etc. While these are important, and even essential ministerial activities, they do not take the place of our processing the ongoing assessments of our leadership effectiveness by our constituents. And this need becomes never more critical than when we are working in multicultural, multiracial, multiethnic, and dually gendered environments. Effective leadership in the twenty-first century requires an awareness, and even the competency to lead across the sub- and co-cultures within our territories.

Our church's diversity makes the idea of limiting cross-cultural training for mission to departing missionaries an antiquated fallacy. For example, every cultural tribe and nation on the globe lives within North America. Just visit New York, Los Angeles, Chicago, or Philadelphia (or Dubuque, Stockton, or Fort Lauderdale). Go abroad and visit Paris,

Nairobi, Geneva, Rome, Hong Kong, or Sydney. In each of the places, we will find an unprecedented association of persons from diverse cultures. Thus, church growth, evangelism, church planting, educational leadership, healthcare training, delivery, teambuilding, as well as a host of other mission-based ministries consist of significant cross-cultural encounters in modern leadership.

Furthermore, as conferences, churches, hospitals, and schools diversify, the issues of multicultural cohesion and partnering in the local conference, union, and division will assume more significance. I am impressed that one of our greatest needs at the beginning of the twenty-first century comprises leadership training at every organizational level that equips our institutions to competently accomplish the mission of the church in our changed demographic situation. This article will provide some knowledge and awareness of some of the dimensions of culture that make our followers diverse. Then some suggestions are made to aid ministerial leaders in achieving effectiveness in their leadership. A full elaboration of the essential knowledge, insights, and skills is laid out in my book on the subject.[2] But first a story.

Ahhhhh, a perfect postcard Thursday afternoon, I think to myself as I stand near the isolated Keekorok airstrip, anticipating the arrival of Air Kenya Flight 422 to Nairobi. Kenya is good for me. She teaches this driven North American how to hurry up and wait. She also teaches me how to enjoy that waiting.

Today I sit amid the peaceful surroundings of Kenya's Masai Mara. My airstrip is an isolated red rock and sand stretch of land about 240 kilometers west of Nairobi in the region known as Keekorok (meaning "place of the black trees," in the Maasai language). This well-utilized landing area rests squarely in the grazing lands of thousands of wildebeests, zebra, Thompson gazelle, and impala. I have arrived during the season of the great migrations in Kenya and as I inhale my surroundings, I am keenly aware that this plain is fraught with both breath-taking beauty and incredible danger. For all of its apparent tranquility, hungry lions, stealthy leopards, and crouching cheetahs lurk within the golden strands of the Mara's grassy knolls.

I sit in Maasai land. Generous and approachable, the Maasai are among Kenya's pastoralists, i.e., herdsmen and shepherds. Their flaming red shawls light up the Mara and warns predators that the Maasai will fight to the death to protect a cow or goat. I cannot help feeling impressed that the Maasai are a proud and beautiful people.

Geoffrey Kulet, my fifty-two-year-old Maasai driver and tour guide, sits quietly beside me. Geoffrey wears a carefully coordinated Safari khaki outfit. A gentle and quiet man of slender stature, Geoffrey seems reluctant to leave my side, since doing so would be considered grossly inhospitable within his Maasai values. Presence with a guest matters, and I am his guest. And me? Like the typical American, I never met a silence that I really liked. So, in an effort to make conversation, I laughingly say to my host, "Hey, Geoffrey, suppose I wanted to become a Maasai man. What would I have to do?"

Geoffrey's gentle eyes widen first; then he laughs heartily. "There is no way *you* could become a Maasai man. You could live on the Maasai land, but you could never be a Maasai man."

"Couldn't I be adopted into the tribe?" I ask.

He laughs even more robustly as he remarks, "It does not work that way."

I respond lightheartedly, "But you are black people, and I am a black person. That should be enough!"

Then in his beautifully accented Kenyan English, Geoffrey says, "We have forty-two tribes of black people in Kenya. Being black is not enough. They cannot be Maasai and you cannot either. It's where you are born and the way you are raised. You are an American." While Geoffrey could point to forty-two tribes in Kenya, I wonder how many racial and cultural "tribes" we have beyond Kenya.

Let's begin by carefully exploring the relationship between race and culture. After one departs from the notion of the existence of only one race—the human race—one must then define race based on biophysical characteristics. The weakness with this approach alone is that pigmentation, hair texture, and physical features have no inherent meaning for the values, outlooks, and attitudes that diverse persons hold. Socialization, acculturation, and choice influence these. That's what Geoffrey was try-ing to say to me in response to my query about an African American becoming a Maasai. Ultimately, subsurface differences—values, beliefs, outlooks—make us who we are and make other people who they are. Culture matters!

Let's define culture. Culture consists of all of the acquired lenses through which we learn to interpret our environment. It includes our beliefs, our values, our mores, our folkways, our language(s), and the expected behaviors from others around us. Culture is that set of beliefs and actions that we use to first, identify ourselves as belonging to a group, and second, to distinguish ourselves from other groups. Culture repre-sents a way of perceiving, behaving, and evaluating one's world. It pro-vides the blueprint or guide for determining and often expressing one's values, beliefs, and practices. Please note the following four characteris-tics of culture:

1. *Culture is learned from birth.* Culture is learned from birth through learning one's primary language and through socialization, or how one is raised. If we were to take three newborn babies, each born to the same mother and father, across three consecutive years, and entrust the first child to a set of parents from Papua, New Guinea, the second child to parents from Bejing, China, and the third child to parents from San Juan, Puerto Rico, in twenty years each of those children would reflect uniquely distinct cultural characteristics. Their socialization would make the substantial difference in their languages, outlooks, and ways of being. From society's viewpoint, socialization can be described as the way cul-ture is passed on, and the individuals fit into a people group's organized way of life.

2. *Members of the same cultural group share it.* In fact, the sharing of cultural beliefs and patterns binds people together under one identity as a group—even though this is not always a conscious process. Shared culture also distinguishes groups from each other.

3. *Culture—an adaptation to specific conditions.* These specific condi-tions relate to environmental and technical factors and to the availability of natural resources. In other words, our culture can be passed on and

modified by the kinds of demands of our environment.

4. Culture—dynamic, not static. Culture, although stable at its roots, on its surface is a dynamic ever-changing process. Expressed in the artifacts, religion, values, beliefs, mores, and assumptions that both define and distinguish people groups, group culture has both macro and micro dimensions.

So what makes our *followership* multicultural and diverse beyond observable bio-physical differences? Values and beliefs make a significant difference. Some of the concepts around which cultural values are formed for our followers consist of a number of turning points. Here are ten questions that you might want to ask your followers:

1. Is deity immediate or distant? Does collective group life assume that deity is immediately involved in its affairs or the deity is distant, detached, and uninvolved?

2. What are the roles and relationship expectations between genders? What are males' primary and secondary responsibilities in the group? What are females' primary and secondary responsibilities in the group? How do males and females rank in relation to each other?

3. How is power accrued and utilized? Can we call power a divine gift? Is it a function of political caprice or familial relationship or biological endowment? Does power flow from top to bottom or from bottom to top?

4. What is the orientation toward past, present, and future? Will the future be better than the past, or was the past more glorious than the future? Is the present to be endured or enjoyed?

5. Is time a chronological or phenomenological reality? Is time discreetly defined by the clock, i.e., is it fluid in its nature? Is time a more diffuse reality marked by historical and social occurrences, i.e., is time a more people- and event-ordered reality? Or is time an external measure of efficiency, for example?

6. What are the boundaries of public, social, and personal space? What are the group's expectations concerning how space between persons and sexes will be managed? Will there be public touch between persons of the opposite gender? When does personal space become intimate? How much space is required for comfort in public between differing "ranks" of persons?

7. *What are the qualifications for insider and outsider status?* How are insiders determined? Can one be more of a cultural insider than another? Who are outsiders? Can outsiders become insiders, and how?

8. *How do talking and touching function?* Is talk primarily for the communication of information, or is it an affirmation of relationship? Is talk direct and precise or narrative and allusive? When and where is touch between acquaintances appropriate?

9. *What is the relationship between individual and group identity?* In achievement, obligation, success, or failure, do the individuals represent themselves primarily or do individuals primarily represent their familial, ethnic, racial, national, and cultural groups?

10. *What is the role and place of formality and informality?* Are titles such as Doctor, Captain, Mr., Mrs., for example, necessary elements of personal address? Does friendship require that titles be dispensed with? Are religious services formal or informal occasions? How quickly can a stranger address someone by their first name? The beliefs formed around these concepts constitute starting points of discussion for the leader wanting to communicate more effectively across cultures. But the leader cannot stop there.

Every leader must do the personal diversity work that will free us to identify and relativize our own culturalness. This personal diversity work requires us to assess the strengths and limitations of our cultural of origin. Too many persons are only vaguely aware of the presence and impact of their culture of origin on their behavior. Tastes in music, dress, concepts of modesty, preferences in attire, and a host of other personal behaviors and outlooks may reflect one's cultural origins. Culture is learned through a process of cultural osmosis in which the values, attitudes, roles, and behaviors acceptable to and expected by the cultural group are absorbed and reflected. This process begins in the family. Parents set examples of correct cultural behavior through their use of praise, punishment, and communication to their children. The larger community also participates in communicating its cultural expectations.

For instance, the values of freedom, independence, and egalitarianism are so deeply imbedded in mainstream American and Canadian cultures that we Americans often assume that these are normative for others. Our reward systems both compensate and validate these values. However, there are many groups for whom interdependence, hierarchy, and collectivism or harmony guide social relations. In other words, many individuals first reference their behavior against their group *prior* to deciding an individual course of action. Effective leadership for mission in today's multicultural marketplace requires new and informed ways of thinking about the various people groups who compose our field, church, and institution, for example. That means that we will need to change our thinking about local mission. George Bernard Shaw was correct when he said, "Progress is impossible without change; and those who cannot change their minds, cannot change anything!" Change is the price we pay for progress, isn't it?

We could and should also explore the relationship of the Bible to *our* group's culture before we presume to do a biblical critique of a follower's culture. The kingdom of God promotes very specific values, such as loyalty to God over every human ordinance (Acts 5:29), denial of self (Matthew 16:24, 25), self-abnegation (Galatians 2:20), sacrificial service to others (Matthew 20:26–28), collective good over individual expression (1 Corinthians 14:1–5), mutual cooperation over competition (1 Corinthians 3:1–9), preference for others over self-elevation (Philippians 2:3), esteem for the socially marginalized (Matthew 25:40, 45), and a host of other values. Leaders who in light of the Bible cannot articulate a biblical critique of their culture of origin's cherished and transmitted values are not qualified to objectively evaluate another culture. Almost without exception, culturally incompetent leaders assume that their culture of origin is superior to the culture under their microscope. Thus, many well-meaning leaders sometimes too easily move to condemn what they view as culturally unacceptable in someone else's cultural group. The following story reminded me of this tendency in each of us. The story should not be construed as support for the worship or veneration of the dead, but the story illustrates the way we often judge the practices of others through our own eyes, and not through what they might see in the eyes of others who are different from us.

A missionary worked among a group of Native Americans in New Mexico at the turn of the century with an assigned task to evangelize this group. Over time he had built a warm rapport with the Native American group, particularly their head chief, Chief Brave Eagle, and his tribal council leaders.

In the course of time, one of the tribal elders, Running Bear, died, and his tribal clan arranged for his funeral. One of Running Bear's tribal customs was for each family to leave a plate of food at the gravesite in memory of their loved one. The missionary was not aware of this custom, and upon arriving at the gravesite, was surprised to see a grave decorated with platters of food. In the missionary's mind, the Native Americans were squandering this perfectly edible food.

Toward the afternoon sunset, after the family and tribal members had departed the gravesite with the food still sitting atop the grave, the missionary was left alone with Chief Brave Eagle. The missionary leaned over and asked the chief, "Chief, when do you think Running Bear will have time to eat all of this food?"

The chief paused, looked heavenward, and after a thoughtful silence replied, "Just about the same time that your dead will have time to smell all those flowers you leave for them." There is something worth thinking about.

Finally, the Christian movement's most prolific and effective cross-culturalist testified that when it comes to mission, culture matters (read 1 Corinthians 9:18–21). A comprehensive program of training for ecclesiastical, healthcare, and educational leadership needs to be organized and launched. Why? Because we train to what we value. We value soul winning; thus we put time, money, and personnel resources in this area. We value stewardship; thus we pay persons to promote stewardship. In short, what we value we pay for; what we pay for, we value. Thus we cannot say that we value diversity in our division if we invest virtually no personnel or monetary resources in maximizing its potential for aiding in mission accomplishment and mutual ministry.

Listen to Ellen G. White: "There is no person, no nation that is perfect in every habit and thought. One must learn of another. Therefore God wants the different nationalities to mingle together, to be one in judgment, one in purpose. Then the union that there is in Christ will be exemplified."[3] Her statement enjoins cross-cultural learning upon the body of Christ. This means that every cultural group can learn from every other group. It also means that every other cultural group can teach every other. Where one group is weak, I assure you another is strong.

Our mission is to go to "every nation, language, tongue, and people." But what should we do when every nation, language, tongue, and people come to us? In cities like New York, Los Angeles, Paris, London, Chicago, Toronto, Montreal, and in all points in between, urbanization brings together diverse people groups in a way previously unprecedented. A reason to organize and launch training is because every leader's skill sets expand with the acquisition of new insights, understandings, and perspectives. And one fact that will not go away is that the twenty-first century demands a generation of leaders who are cross-culturally competent. Our greatest need is for leaders of spiritual maturity and personal security who see in every diverse person a candidate for the kingdom.

So what can a leader do to create a positive diversity climate in their organization? Five suggested actions follow:

1. Promote awareness. Be the diversity leader in your church institution. We leaders set the inclusivity temperature of our organization. Remember: diversity responsiveness is a follow-the-leader activity. One leadership expert said, "Leaders communicate their priorities, values, and concerns by their choice of things to ask about, measure, comment on, praise, and criticize."[4] Ask your leadership team the following question that I like to ask my colleagues: "What are we doing to serve the diverse people in our field, institution, union, and hospital?" Others will follow your lead when it comes to diversity!

2. To ensure responsibility, require accountability. Colleagues, I have found that in leadership, we rarely get what we expect, but we generally receive what we inspect. Our colleagues in healthcare know that counting the numbers really matters. If we want to diversify our working boards and teams, start counting how much representation we have and from where. Very quickly, a picture will emerge. If we like that picture, then our work is done. If we are dissatisfied with that picture, then we can begin collaborating and planning in intentional ways to supplement, modify, or correct the picture.

3. Provide diversity education. Training helps followers understand the power of surface and subsurface differences. While traveling to Lagos, Nigeria, recently, my clothes were mistakenly sent to Cairo, Egypt. I was given some beautiful and colorful Nigerian garments to wear. Then my host said to me, "Dr. Pollard, let's go to town center in Lagos so that you can see the city." And that we did. While there, a Nigerian street child and his little friend approached me with his upturned palm and began speaking in Yoruba (a tribal language of western Nigeria). I decided to play along by nodding as if I understood his attempts to get me to give him a donation. After about two minutes of entertaining his best and most animated appeals, I finally said to him, "I am so sorry, but I don't understand a word you are saying." At the sound of my American accent, a smile crawled across his face as he turned to his little companion and giggled in perfect English, "Hurry, hurry!" he said. "Come meet the black white man!" In that moment, my little friend's quick and comical analysis revealed a profound anthropological insight. Subsurface differences make the difference—educate to these differences.

4. Diversify your leadership committees. Homogenous committees are not broad, rich, or deep enough to maximize our service effectiveness. Are any disabled people on your leadership team? In places where physical disability earns such stigma, this is vital. How many women are in your councils? When there was organized opposition along ethnic or racial lines to your election, did you reach out to the opposition?

5. Mentor across gender, racial, and cultural lines. Were I to ask you, "Who are you mentoring across racial, cultural, or gender lines," what would be your answer? Find someone who is not like you and offer them the gift of your mentoring.

Conclusion

Revelation 7:9 reminds us that heaven will be a multinational, multi-racial, cosmopolitan place. I once did a series of diversity presentations in a major European city where, in a sea of Anglo persons, I was the only black person in the building. The audience's level of interaction impressed me that they were quite receptive to the presentations on diversity that I was conducting. And the group had very good and very honest questions that we discussed in light of our scriptural mission.

Now, I do not know why I did the next thing, but I did. I smile now as I think that either the Holy Spirit moved me or I succumbed to low-impulse control. At the end of the meeting right after the benediction, I took the mike and asked, "How many of you have never hugged a black person? Please raise your hands." At first a few brave souls raised their hands. I then said, "Good, come on down to the front so I can help get you ready for heaven." A chorus of laughter arose and then, wonder of wonders, people, older and younger, people that I had met for the first time, people who lived in rural areas, literally lined up to hug and bid me farewell and safe travel back to California! Trite, you might think. But hold on a moment. Does not the plowing of a new furrow begin with the first break of the soil? And does not the falling of the tree begin with the first cut? And does not the collapse of the sturdiest wall begin with its first crevice?

Listen to Ellen G. White again when she says, "The walls of sectarianism and caste and race will fall down when the true missionary spirit enters the hearts of men. Prejudice is melted away by the love of God."[5] Heaven's reach-back effect begins the transformation of our present reality (Hebrews 6:16). Leaders, we can help make this a reality where we serve.

I attend workshops and corporate training where, despite spending large amounts of money, diversity gurus struggle with these concepts of mission and inclusion. But Ellen White reminds us of the advantage God offers to His community of faith. She says, "Christ tears away the wall of partition, the self-love, the dividing prejudice of nationality, and teaches a love for all the human family. He lifts men from the narrow circle that their selfishness prescribes; He abolishes all territorial lines and artificial distinctions of society. He makes no difference between neighbors and strangers, friends and enemies. He teaches us to look upon every needy soul as our neighbor and the world as our field."[6] Our greatest resource lies in the love of God bathed in a thorough knowledge of how culture impacts group and personal behavior. Let's take advantage of the resources God has granted to us. And let's do it now.

1. Mary L. Connerly and Paul Pederson, *Leadership in a Diverse and Multicultural Environment: Developing Awareness, Knowledge, and Skills* (Thousand Oaks, CA: Sage Publications, 2005), ix. Geert Hofstede quoted.

2. See Leslie N. Pollard, ed., *Embracing Diversity: How to Reach People of All Cultures* (Hagerstown, MD: Review and Herald® Publishing Association, 2000). This book contains insider explanations of how particular cultures look at the world. Chapter authors from a variety of backgrounds show readers how to understand previously misunderstood or unknown facts and features of other cultural groups.

3. Ellen G. White, *Historical Sketches of the Foreign Missions of the Seventh-day Adventists* (Basle: Imprimerie Polyglotte, 1886), 137.

4. Gary Yukl, *Leadership in Organizations* (New Jersey: Prentice Hall, 1985), 213.

5. Ellen G. White, *The Southern Work* (Washington, DC: Review and Herald® Publishing Association, 1966), 55.

6. Ellen G. White, *Thoughts From the Mount of Blessing* (Mountain View, CA: Pacific Press® Publishing Association), 42.

Chapter 14

Living Before God:
The Pastor and Ethics

Nikolaus Satelmajer

"She made me do it," and other excuses

The treasurer of a well-known denomination was paid about three times more than a pastor in the same denomination. Although with her salary she could live a very comfortable life, later it came out that she had embezzled the equivalent of nearly *twenty* times her annual salary.

Not only did she steal the money from her church, she also refused to accept responsibility for her actions. During legal proceedings, her attorney blamed her actions on faulty memory. Testifying on her behalf, a psychiatrist explained that her actions were the result of bipolar mood disorder.[1] Both explanations avoided the central issue—her behavior was wrong. It was unethical.

Sexual misconduct can be classified as another form of unethical behavior. All too often, the very individuals who should be trusted commit sexual misconduct.

Accused of having sexual contact with a thirteen-year-old girl, a city police chief blamed the young girl for the occurrences. Asked by the prosecutor, "Couldn't you have said no?" the chief of police responded that "he couldn't then but he's getting better at it."[2] Imagine: an adult man in a position of great authority blaming a minor for his actions.

Some ministers who claim to have committed their lives to the Lord Jesus Christ and who call upon others to follow Jesus have engaged in sexual misconduct. Studies show that Roman Catholic priests are more often involved in sexual misconduct with children, whereas other clergy (Protestant, Jewish, and Muslim) most often are involved in sexual misconduct with adults.[3] Whether with children or adults, misconduct is still wrong. Clergy engaged in such misconduct are not faithful to God—and they roam among the flock and the community as predators.

"How widespread is clergy misconduct?" you ask. Some people say, "It may be happening in other denominations, but not among us." But how do they know that to be so? Is it just a hopeful assumption? Some authorities have estimated that up to 10 percent of clergy are involved in some form of sexual misconduct.[4] The church should not tolerate any level of sexual misconduct by ministers—or by anyone else for that matter.

What can be done about clergy who are involved in sexual misconduct? In some instances, leaders do take appropriate action, but all too often, even the leadership starts shifting the blame elsewhere. One researcher writes that the perception exists that all too often church policy is modeled on "Forgive and forget—forgive the perpetrator and forget the victim."[5]

In reality, members are starting to call for accountability from ministers who are involved in improper behavior (sexual, financial, power, etc.). At a convention for victims of sexual misconduct, an organization that addresses the issue of Protestant and Catholic clergy abuse hung a banner with the names of 666 priests involved in sexual abuse. When asked why, the leaders responded, "We have many more names, but the number's theologically significant. And we ran out of room to include more names."[6]

We may be tempted to conclude that abuse does not happen in our country or our denomination. But before we become too defensive, we need to ask ourselves, *Do we know the facts?* If an organization like the one cited had access to all of our records, how many and which names would they list?

We must recognize some of the underlying reasons for such improper behavior. William Schweiker has written a helpful book that helps us understand fundamental changes that have occurred in our societies and thus in our own lives. Read carefully this insight from Schweiker: "Finally, contemporary ethics in the West face the loss of the influence of Jewish and Christian theism on our culture in terms of the source of value. . . . The point is that we have lost metaphysical, anthropological, and theological means for providing norms for life, for grounding in moral identity, and for interpreting moral terms. With this loss, I have been arguing, power becomes the central value and the maximizing of power becomes the purpose of human existence."[7]

Schweiker reminds us that if we ignore God, we lose the norms that provide reference points for behavior. In such an environment, whatever I desire I have a right to get. Or if I have power to get it, it is mine. Thus, desire and power govern behavior.

The source of our ethics?

What are the practical implications of leaving God out of our lives? Among other things, it means that God does not govern our behavior. The *Humanist Manifestos I and II* follows the idea of leaving out God to its logical conclusion when it states that "Ethics is *autonomous* and *situational*, needing no theological or ideological sanction."[8] The consequences of such a position are far-reaching: it means that *we* decide what is right or wrong, and each decision depends on the situation. As one writer states, "Recent decades have been marked by widespread rejection of biblical teachings and norms."[9]

Walking away from God's norms can bring us to the point where no rights or wrongs exist. Under such circumstances, power becomes the deciding factor. We turn again to Schweiker to remind us of the implications of these changes. "Modern ethics does not understand the human as the *image of God,* but as a product of evolutionary processes, social relations, or discrete acts of freedom. This means that the central question becomes the status of power . . . and this raises basic moral questions. Does power determine what is right such that the strong ought to dominate the weak."[10]

It is not surprising that in popular culture, we hear the comment that "you have to be true to yourself." That may seem to be appealing, but realistically, it has no value when it comes to our behavior. There are many who are "true to themselves" and commit horrible wrongs. Think of some of the despotic and violent dictators our world has seen. They have been "true to themselves," but that does not make their actions right. Murderers, adulterers, thieves, sexual molesters—they may be "true to themselves," but their actions are evil. Should you be "true to yourself"? Yes, but only if *self* is being guided by God.

If we are not the source of ethical norms, what is the source? God's Word is the source—we are accountable to God. "And whatever you do, whether in word or deed, do it all in the name of the Lord Jesus, giving thanks to God the Father through him" (Colossians 3:17, NIV).

Paul does not leave out anyone. In the previous verses, he gives various exhortations, but "Finally these general injunctions are summed up in an exhortation of universal scope, covering every aspect of life."[11] As ministers, we call upon others to live a new life. And we, too, are called upon to live the new life. Paul challenges ministers to be examples: "Don't let anyone look down on you because you are young, but set an example for the believers in speech, in life, in love, in faith and in purity" (1 Timothy 4:12, NIV).

We not only live our lives before others, but more importantly, we live our lives before God.[12] Once we realize this, and that we need the grace of God, we are on an ethical journey. For this journey to be successful, we must recognize that ethics is much more than outward behavior, for ethics deals with character. Harmony must exist between our theology and our lives. As Brian K. Blount writes, "In Paul, theology and ethics always go together."[13] With both a challenge and an invitation, Ellen White wrote, "Let him [the minister] show to others that the truth has done something for him."[14] David, after committing grievous offenses against humans and God, cries out for help from God. Once he recognized the sinfulness of his character, he asked God to wash, cleanse, create, and restore him (Psalm 51). The offender must be re-created by the Creator.

Ethics in the daily life of the pastor

The pastor faces ethical issues every day.

Preaching. William Willimon, in his book on the work of pastors, reminds us that "Preaching is ethically demanding."[15] Not only the sharing of information, preaching includes telling what the Lord Jesus Christ is doing in our lives, so that the hearers will realize that they, too, can experience the new life in Christ.

Private life. What pastor does not crave for some privacy? Yet privacy, which is needed, does not take away accountability.[16] Practically speaking, we cannot separate our public and private lives because the private person is reflected in the public life.

Family relationships. Many pastors do not treat their families as being very important. Yet we are reminded that "The spiritual welfare of [the pastor's] family comes first."[17] As if not challenging enough, the same writer states that "It is not so much the religion of the pulpit as the religion of the family that reveals our real character."[18] After all, which is more difficult: preach a sermon or apologize to your spouse, daughter, or son? Some of us would probably rather prepare and preach a series of sermons before offering an apology.

Those of us who are married should remember how we treated our spouses before the marriage. Prior to marriage, we tended to be more gracious, understanding, forgiving, and always looking for reasons to compliment the other. We need those positive attitudes and behaviors to strengthen our families.

Relationships with other pastors. Remember the first days of that new assignment? Some said that you were more capable or a better preacher than your predecessor. Noel S. Fraser, who has held various ministerial roles in the West Indies, reminds us that, "The same tongue that curses our predecessor will also curse you when the time comes."[19] We can be successful and effective without allowing ourselves to be compared to those before and after us. Success is ultimately God's assessment of how faithful we are to our calling.

Our denomination. Because I am a Seventh-day Adventist minister, I write from that perspective. Seventh-day Adventist churches are part of a worldwide organizational structure, and if I choose to be a part of the ministry in this denomination, I have certain ethical responsibilities to it. If I mercilessly criticize my denomination, why should I be surprised if the members of my church follow that example and criticize me?

Counseling ministry. While pastoral counseling is a part of ministry, most pastors do not have the expertise or the time to do general counseling. Pastoral counseling may take place during a brief conversation in church or in a more formal meeting at an appropriate place. Because all pastoral counseling requires adherence to strict professional standards, here are some helpful principles which will help you, as a pastor, avoid some dangerous pitfalls. Recognize your limitations.

1. *Limited time.* Consider pastoral counseling as only one part of ministry.
2. *Limited expertise.* Pastors cannot address all of the issues, as experts, that members face.
3. *Limited understanding of facts.* Although tempting to listen to a person give an account of the actions or words of another person and reach conclusions, how does the pastor know the accuracy of the report? Before we reach conclusions about the person not present, we need to hear from that person.

Seeking a resolution. Pastors should recognize the importance of working toward resolution; otherwise, very little will be accomplished. Here are some suggested principles to keep in mind:

1. *Listen.* Listening is difficult but necessary if we want to help the member look for a resolution.
2. *Focus.* Some individuals want to spend most of the time retelling wrongs done to them or recounting their hurts. While the pastor should recognize the importance of listening to past events, focusing on solutions should be considered critical. For example, asking a person to consider their options will help them focus on a resolution.
3. *Refer.* Some situations need the attention of other counselors or healthcare workers, but only refer those individuals to professionals you are sure are competent and ethical.

4. *Confidentiality.* Carelessness with confidential information will harm the member and bring the work of the minister into question.
5. *Legal implications.* On occasion, an individual will share information that has legal implications, and ministers should know their responsibility. For example, what do you do with information about sexual abuse of a minor?

Sexual issues. Sexual issues will come up during pastoral counseling with devastating consequences if a pastor takes advantage of such situations. Ellen G. White appropriately refers to such instances as taking advantage of the confidence which is placed in the pastor.[20] Self-confidence and power are two reasons why pastors cross the line that should never be crossed.

What are some specific steps for pastors to take to be faithful to the sacred work to which God has called them?

Be in love with your spouse and let others know it. Are you and your spouse seen together? Do others see the bond that exists between you and your spouse so that when you are seen together, a positive message is given?

1. *Be aware of your vulnerability.* Yes, it *can* happen to you.
2. *Be accountable.* Accountability to another person will help the minister stay away from improper relationships. But, remember, we are not only accountable to others—our accountability is ultimately to God.
3. *Be ready to run.* Instances occur when the pastor must exercise the Joseph option—run. The pastor will come into contact with individuals who are not interested in counseling, but rather desire to enter into an immoral relationship.
4. *Be spiritually strong.* Pastors must have an ongoing plan for spiritual growth. What is yours?

Planning to act ethically

All too often, the discussion of pastoral ethics happens *after* a serious problem has occurred. This section will help pastors order their lives in such a way that they will not be party to serious ethical problems. Here are some specific actions:

Address the problem. Admitting that a problem exists is important but not sufficient. A well-known writer and storyteller describes a bar scene with a song being played. "A tangy song played on the jukebox, the deep, mournful voice of a man *sorry for his misdeeds while still committing them.*"[21] How sorry was the singer for his misdeeds if he was still committing them? How sorry is a pastor who acknowledges a wrong but continues doing it? Do not detour around the problem. Deal with it.

Bypass the first desire. Schweiker states that "All of us have first-order sexual desires."[22] We may want to call such desires temptations, but temptations in themselves are not sin. Having a desire is not sufficient ground for acting upon it. The question is, Do we allow it to grow to the point at which we act upon it?

Describe. Describe your actions or relationships to another individual—I mean the actions you would rather not talk about. If you are not bold enough to describe them to a confidant, challenge yourself to at least write them down. Write down something such as: "[Name of person] and I are ..." How would you complete such a sentence? What are you and that person talking about, planning, and doing? Would you feel comfortable describing it to others? If not, change course.

Follow the road. Where is the road on which you are traveling taking you? Look ahead and acknowledge where you are heading, for good intentions alone will not help us if we are traveling on the wrong road. Personal feelings do not make the wrong road the right road.

Invite God before disaster strikes. God will listen to our pleas even when we are in the midst of personal disaster. But during this time, while we are in the midst of a disaster of our doing, our spiritual reference points may have disappeared. We should recognize the importance of asking God for spiritual strength before much time passes. Paul says it effectively: "Put on the full armor of God" (Ephesians 6:11–17, NIV).

Dietrich Bonhoeffer wrote that "Morning prayer determines the day."[23] That sums it up well.

1. Anson Shupe, ed., *Wolves Within the Fold: Religious Leadership and Abuses of Power* (New Brunswick, NJ: Rutgers University Press, 1998), 52.

2. *The Chronicle-Herald* (Halifax, Nova Scotia), July 4, 2002.

3. Shupe, *Wolves Within the Fold,* 175.

4. Stanley J. Grenz and Roy D. Bell, *Betrayal of Trust: Confronting and Preventing Clergy Sexual Misconduct* (Grand Rapids, MI: Baker Books, 1995), 23.

5. Shupe, *Wolves Within the Fold,* 24.

6. Ibid., 230, 231.

7. William Schweiker, *Responsibility and Christian Ethics* (Cambridge: Cambridge University Press, 1999), 192, 193.

8. Paul Kurtz, ed., *Humanist Manifestos I and II* (Buffalo: Prometheus Books, 1977), 17; italics in original.

9. Grenz and Bell, *Betrayal of Trust: Confronting and Preventing Clergy Sexual Misconduct,* 76.

10. Schweiker, *Responsibility and Christian Ethics,* 73.

11. F. F. Bruce, *The Epistles to the Colossians, to Philemon and to the Ephesians* (Grand Rapids, MI: William B. Eerdmans, 1984), 139.

12. See Schweiker, *Responsibility and Christian Ethics,* 3, for expansion of this theme.

13. Brian K. Blount, *Then the Whisper Put on Flesh: New Testament Ethics in an African American Context* (Nashville: Abingdon Press, 2001), 125.

14. Ellen G. White, *Pastoral Ministry,* 55.

15. William Willimon, *Pastor* (Nashville, Abingdon Press, 2002), 159.

16. For further discussion, see David Hadley, "Where Judgement Begins," *Leadership,* Winter 2003.

17. White, *Pastoral Ministry,* 85.

18. Ibid.

19. Lecture delivered January 29, 1998.

20. White, *Pastoral Ministry,* 59.

21. Garrison Keeler, *Wobegon Boy* (New York: Penguin Boos, 1997), 173; italics supplied.

22. Schweiker, *Responsibility and Christian Ethics,* 170, 171.

23. Willimon, *Pastor,* 327.

Chapter 15

The Pastor and Financial Stewardship

Jonas Arrais

Stewardship includes many aspects of life, and finances, of course, can be listed as one of those areas. Pastors give the leadership needed so that the financial resources needed for the mission of the church are provided.

A pastor wisely administers, in consultation with the church board, the financial resources of the church, has a well-planned budget, and motivates faithfulness and generosity among the church members. Pastors who neglect these tasks will have a church that reflects their leadership style. In fact, the ministry of pastors will not be successful as long as they lead churches with financial problems.

Many churches believe they have a good pastor, but if they do not have enough funds to finance their own basic needs, their pastor may not be as good as they may think. The financial poverty of many churches may also reflect poor administration of funds by the local church leaders. Whatever the cause, the problem must be resolved for church members to experience heaven's blessings.

In my opinion, no such thing as a poor church exists—just poor leadership. A good pastor may have a simple church, but not a poor church. One great difference between a poor church and a simple church can be listed as a lack of financial resources for almost everything in a poor church, while in a simple church there are financial resources for basic needs.

A poor church does not represent the name of God well, for our Lord abounds in riches, not poverty. God loves the poor and has compassion toward the needy, but He abominates poverty because of its relation to the existence of sin. We should remember that we have a God who bestows rich, great, and good gifts upon His children.

When local leaders seek their pastor or the church treasurer to request funds to buy materials for their departments, and the only answer they hear is "We have no money," the church begins to create a culture of poverty. Remember, God can bless a congregation by increasing its income or reducing its expenses.

While the majority of the members may be faithful in returning their tithes, their response may not always be the same when giving offerings. In many places, the members are accustomed to giving charity donations instead of giving offerings that reflect the blessings they have received from God. One day a couple was returning from church with their young son when the husband mentioned that he did not like the pastor's sermon. His wife took opportunity to criticize the quality of the music. The son, who had observed his father's offering, responded, "And for that small offering, did you expect anything better?" The church usually gives back in direct relationship to what the members have offered it.

The fable of the one dollar bill encountering the fifty dollar bill illustrates the reality in too many of our churches. The dollar bill asked, "Where have you been that I haven't seen you in a long time?" With great pride, the fifty dollar bill responded, "I have been in the banks, casinos, good restaurants, and sometimes I've even gone abroad. And where have *you* been?" "Well, I have been around the churches—Adventist, Baptist, Presbyterian . . ." The dollar bill went on and on, mentioning different churches. Somewhat surprised, the fifty dollar bill asked, "Please forgive my ignorance, but what is a church? I have never been to such a place."

As I visited a church one day when the offering plate came by, I placed in it a twenty dollar bill. The deacon looked at me surprised, and asked how much change I wanted back. It must have been a long time since the deacon last saw a twenty dollar bill in the offering plate. At some churches, I notice the members giving donations to other entities instead of offerings, and I feel that their pastor is not doing much to improve the situation.

Practical steps

The following practical steps can help your church increase the offerings received at your next church service. These concepts are of great value, especially for those pastors who may have been forgetting to practice these details.

1. Ask the most dynamic person on the worship team to announce tithes and offerings. This does not happen in most churches where I've been. Generally, the greatest concern of the platform coordinator, when assigning tasks, centers around who will offer the pastoral prayer. (We are not including for this discussion the person who will deliver the sermon.) After the preacher, the person who will invite the worshipers to give has the most difficult task. Only tradition leads us to assume that the person who offers the pastoral prayer has a greater challenge. Of course, leading the congregation in meaningful prayer is important, but many of the members can do that.

To announce tithes and offerings, however, becomes a much more complex task and requires more ability. We must not assume it is an easy task for just any member to fulfill. To communicate to the congregation that this is the most important responsive moment in our worship to God, to motivate the worshipers to be generous, and to explain the great benefits of such resources for the church, requires deeper skills than presenting a public prayer.

One Sabbath at a church where I was invited to preach, as the platform coordinator gave the different assignments to the people participating in the worship service, he confirmed my participation by saying, "Pastor, you will have the sermon and the closing prayer." I was curious to find out who he would assign to announce the offering. He looked at a man who seemed to be a qualified speaker and said, "Brother, you will offer the pastoral prayer."

Then, after he had made several other assignments, he finally approached a seemingly very timid young lady and said, "You will announce tithes and offerings."

"Who, me?" she asked, quite surprised. "What am I supposed to say?"

The coordinator replied, "Well, read Malachi chapter three, verse ten."

The young lady did her very best, but it was far from what it should have been. Such appeals, presented without adequate preparation or due motivation, result in a collection of monies just as poor as the invitation.

At the church where I recently served as pastor, I tried to develop the habit of thanking each person who participated in leading the worship service. I particularly liked to show appreciation and to thank those who developed some important activity in the church. I instructed the worship coordinator to always choose the person with better speaking ability to announce the offerings. On some occasions, I even asked the participants whether they felt secure and calm about the assignment they were to perform. Often, I would instruct them, or even expand on what they would say as they made the announcement. The worship platform coordinators should have this kind of concern regardless of the size of the congregation.

As I visited a church, I felt frustrated to see how unprepared and unmotivated the person was who announced the offering at the church service. As a result, while the deacons distributed the offering plates, I observed that less than 10 percent of the worshipers were giving. When the deacons came forward for the prayer of gratitude, the offering plates were almost empty. Motivated to repair what the earlier offering announcement had lacked, I asked the congregation, "Are you all aware that you came to this place today to worship God? Do you know that a very important part of our worship to God is the act of giving offerings? Are you aware of the benefits that this offering will bring to your church and to the preaching of the gospel? I don't know whether the deacons passed the offering plates too quickly for all of you to have opportunity to give, but you must not miss the blessing. So I am asking the pianist to play the offertory again, and the deacons, please, to walk more slowly down the aisles, placing the offering plates in each worshiper's hands so that everyone has opportunity to worship God at this time." After a few minutes, the deacons returned to the front with the offering plates overflowing. Is this church merely a reflection of inadequate leadership?

Choosing the person with the best speaking ability and giving them correct orientation may result, not only in a more dynamic and attractive worship service, but may also provide the worshipers greater motivation to give offerings. I believe this procedure would forever eliminate those monotonous readings that are traditionally endured at every worship service, and would give an opportunity for witnessing or announcements that are more natural and spontaneous.

2. Those who are part of the platform should set an example at the offering time. This does not happen in many churches. Once, a deacon started collecting the offering from the platform. The person who announced the offering had asked the congregation to be generous but did not give anything himself. The deacon was so disappointed that he turned the plate upside down, made a "negative" sign with the other hand, and said, "Today, no one on the platform gave anything." What a shame for those worship leaders!

The church is a reflection of its leadership. When worship leaders do not participate at the offering time, the church follows their example. In the churches where I was a pastor, I would ask those who were going to participate in the worship service if each one had brought their offerings. There were always those who would say, "Oh, pastor, I forgot." I used to say, "No problem, I have five dollars for you. You may give it as offering, but don't forget, you should repay me after sunset."

I didn't need more than two or three Sabbaths for this approach. Soon, the participants in other services learned to prepare their offering. In time, a new habit was created at that church that whoever went to the platform had to give an offering. One day a church brother told me, "Pastor, I don't agree with this. I give my 'planned offering' and I have a monthly offering plan."

"That's good!" I answered. "If all church members were monthly plan givers, there would certainly be no financial problems in the church. But, who in the congregation knows you are a monthly giver? Only the treasurer and yourself. Look, you may continue being a monthly giver, but couldn't you give an extra offering every time you go to the platform? This way, you would be contributing to promote the members' participation at the offering time and no one would conclude that you are unresponsive or nonparticipative, if they observe that you are not giving any offering during the worship service."

He answered, "Very well, pastor, if this helps the members become more generous, every time I go to the platform, I will give an extra offering, but please, don't invite me to the platform every Sabbath."

3. Train the deacons at your church. With deacons qualified and properly trained, the results are visible throughout worship service. I was in one church where at the offering time a deacon approached me, put the offering plate in my hands, and when I gave an offering, he smiled and politely said, "Thank you." I had never seen or heard that before. I was so impressed and happy that I almost asked for the plate back so I could give more money. Here are some additional suggestions that have helped in my ministry.

a. Choose the friendlier deacons to collect the offering. Some deacons are shy. They are good for opening and closing the church door, turning the lights on and off, but not for personal relationships or collecting the offering. Some deacons are not friendly when collecting the offering, or they appear too reserved or serious, as though they had a fight with their spouse or were baptized in lemon juice. Appoint only deacons who are appropriate for this job. Deacons are the church's postcard; therefore, they should be carefully selected and thoroughly oriented.

b. Instruct the deacons to place the offering plate in the worshipers' hands. This creates a positive impact, because church members need to feel when the plate is full or empty. Something spiritual happens when a member receives the offering plate in their own hands. This encourages the worshiper to say, "Lord, here I am to worship You, and here is part of the blessing You have given me." This is beautiful. When the plate goes to other hands, the person receiving it says, "Lord, I also am here to worship You, but today I didn't bring anything." What a sad worship! But what a tremendous motivation to plan for the next time.

c. Use a proper offering container. In some churches with appropriately dressed and well-trained deacons, the offering plate does not seem appropriate for the occasion—some are too small while others are too old. Once I observed that a church's offering plate looked like dessert plates. They were too small, and the involuntary thought came to my mind that the plate was only the size of the leaders' vision. I wondered, *How will the members contribute generously without enough space to put the offerings and where no one sees what the other offered, and how will the members hold the plate without the risk of it accidentally falling from their hands?* A simple and practical example that I have seen in some churches has a velvet fabric covering the offering basket with an elastic circular opening.

d. Establish a beautiful worship. Deacons should be instructed and trained regarding the worship procedures. Establish an appropriate way for their entrance and the places where each should attend. Every offering should be collected starting with the platform participants for an example to be followed by the congregation. While collecting the offering, the deacons do not need to be mechanical or slow. There should be enough deacons to quickly attend the whole congregation, including the gallery or side rooms.

e. Include appropriate music. At some churches, the same offering hymn has been sung for so many years that it no longer impacts the worshipers' minds. An appropriate vocal or instrumental song may be performed to prepare the heart of the worshipers for this solemn moment of the service. And there should be a moment of prayer both for the worshipers and for the purpose to which the offering will be utilized.

One thing is certain: when we take care of specific details in the worship service and when the leader is attentive to improve the worship, the members respond more positively to any appeal and feel they are a vital part of the worship service as well as the church's mission.

Increasing the church offering ten times more

At least two occasions occur during the year when this financial miracle may happen, and one is at the church's anniversary. Do you know when your church celebrates its anniversary? When I pose this question at pastoral councils, most pastors confess they do not know. The few who know confess that they do not plan anything special on that date.

One of the first questions I ask when going to a new church is, "When is the anniversary of this church?" In one church, no one knew the answer. I even asked the older members and still no one knew the date. Then I said, "No one here knows the church's anniversary, right? But I, who am just now arriving as your pastor, do know the date."

The members asked, "You know the date? Then tell us?"

I answered, "It's the first Sabbath of August."

The members were impressed with my knowledge. Actually, I didn't know the date either, but in a place where no one knows the date, the best thing a pastor who's just arriving to lead the church can do, would be to create a date. Of course, I later confessed my sin to the members, justifying the ruse that since no one knew it, I was led to create that date. Even now, they are celebrating the church anniversary on that date.

Every congregation should know and celebrates its anniversary date. This becomes a good occasion to motivate members to a deeper commitment with God as well as the opportune moment to stimulate members to give a special offering. I've always tried to communicate this event in advance by instructing the members that on the coming anniversary day, we will have a special service, special guests, and a beautiful program. Along with my laity leaders, I plan a beautiful, spiritual feast for the entire Sabbath, ending the day with a pleasing social activity. I usually prepare and distribute in advance an envelope with the following words: "My anniversary gift to the church." Thus I motivate the members to prepare a special offering for this special occasion. I explain that this is not a day to give an ordinary offering; I challenge each one of them to prepare a significant offering as an expression of love and gratitude for their church.

The members are reminded that on a birthday, no one gives an insignificant gift to anyone. I illustrate this by saying that when my wife celebrates her birthday, I always try to give her an outstanding gift according to my financial situation to express my love for her. I never give her just a one dollar or a five dollar gift on her birthday because I believe she deserves more. Why then, when we celebrate the church's anniversary, do we think differently to give so little? I explain to my members that their gifts should match what the church represents to them and to their family.

On the church anniversary date, the members feel something different in the air. They are happy to see special details in a well-planned and attractive program. I know that if I prepare a feast with poor details, the members will answer in the same way at the offering time. We prepare several big and beautiful gift boxes in which the members can place their offerings. On this day, the deacons do not collect the offering as they usually do because gratitude is not something you go after, it is something you bring. It inspires everyone to see all the members coming to the front, each one with their envelope, to deposit their gratitude offering in these extraordinary gift boxes.

Then, when the treasurers count the offering after the service, what a surprise! If on a normal Sabbath the offering totals around three thousand dollars, on this anniversary Sabbath, it reaches thirty thousand. It is sad to see churches undergoing financial problems and yet not celebrating this special day.

The second occasion when we can take a similar offering happens on Christmas Day. Again, I usually prepare another envelope, with the following words: "My Christmas gift to my church." In almost every culture, gifts are exchanged at this occasion as an expression of love and kindness. Parents offer gifts to their children, couples and friends exchange gifts with each other. Why not give a special gift to my church? Usually at the end of the year, a greater spirit of generosity and gratitude exists in people's hearts. Let us not miss the opportunity of motivating the members to give a generous offering for the church on such a special occasion.

Ellen G. White comments that, "God would be well pleased if on Christmas each church would have a Christmas tree on which shall be hung offerings, great and small, for these houses of worship."[1] With this idea, we place a beautiful Christmas tree at the front of the church at the beginning of the season. Thus the members are visually reminded each week of the upcoming spiritual response. Then we prepare a special service for the Sabbath of Christmas Day. At the offering time, we invite each member to come individually with their envelope and place it on the tree. Members do this with joy and a profound spirit of gratitude.

Again, at the end of the service when the treasurer counts the offering, what a pleasant surprise! If on a regular Sabbath we collect three thousand dollars of offering, on this day it reaches thirty thousand—nothing less than ten times greater than a regular Sabbath. The treasurer of the church used to get very excited and say, "This is wonderful, pastor! Please create more feasts for this church!" I know that the Seventh-day Adventist Church doesn't work this way, and this spirit does not guide our church programs, but many times I ask myself, *Why do some pastors not value these excellent occasions to raise needed resources for our churches to accomplish their projects?*

When I evaluate the ministerial success of any pastor, some important questions automatically come to my mind. *Are the members appreciating the pastor's preaching? Are the members being trained, equipped, and motivated to accomplish a specific ministry that matches their own spiritual gift? Are they being served with a systematic pastoral visitation program? Is the pastor an administrator who maintains a good relationship with the members and the close cooperation of the laity leaders? Is the church financially healthy?* Each pastor, called by God to develop a ministry in his church, must intentionally be attentive to these important areas of ministerial life.

Then, with the members of a church faithful to God, with the financial resources correctly administered by its leaders, with the giving opportunities carefully planned and well executed, and with the resources needed to provide the growth of the church in all areas available, you will certainly enjoy a financially healthy church.

---

1. Ellen G. White, *The Adventist Home,* 482.

Chapter 16

The Pastor as a Shepherd

Abraham J. Jules, Steve D. Cassimy, D. Robert Kennedy

Pastoring is about shepherding

This chapter restates one of the most obvious truths concerning pastoral leadership, namely, that pastoring does not center around great plans, programs, or policies, as much as around people. The pastor, who liked everything about pastoring except the people, had a profound misunderstanding of the meaning of pastoring. The people of God, for whom Scripture uses the metaphor of "sheep" or "flock"[1] are always in need of shepherding. This explains why one of the most dominant scriptural models for God the Father and Jesus Christ the Son is that of Shepherd. In the Old Testament, the Father is "the Shepherd" (cf. Psalm 23); in the New Testament, the Son is "the Good Shepherd" (see John 10:11, 14), or "the Chief Shepherd" (1 Peter 5:4, KJV).

In both Testaments, those called to be shepherds have to understand themselves as undershepherds (cf. Jeremiah 3:15; 23:4; 10:21; 23:2; Ezekiel 34:2, 7, 8; 1 Peter 5:2). In a larger frame, pastors are identified as both shepherd and sheep. Every child of God who understands the shepherd-sheep relation recites, "The LORD is my shepherd" (Psalm 23:1, KJV). The book of Revelation presents Christ Himself as both Shepherd and Lamb (Revelation 7:17). Christ is leader and fulfiller of the will of God or leader and follower. The fundamental point is that pastors are shepherds and subsidiary sheep—the shepherd leads and also follows.

169

Shepherding focuses attention on "leading and feeding," as Professor Kenneth Gangel correctly puts it in a title of one of his books, *Feeding and Leading*.[2] Since much has been stated on the issue of leading throughout the previous chapters, this chapter focuses on the issue of feeding or nurturing.

Nurturing, as we understand it, leads in the direction of offering knowledge and understanding to the flock,[3] giving oversight, being supportive, offering care and compassion, mediating between fighting sheep, bringing necessary correction to errant sheep, and offering prayerful intercession on behalf of the sheep.

The character of the shepherd

Before further discussion on what a shepherd does, we point to some of the most significant qualities that make for good shepherding—namely the love, kindness, compassion, commitment, and courage that form the two sides of the shepherd's character. Like the holy character of God, the character of the shepherd is full of love and holy courage. In the fifty-first chapter of the *The Acts of the Apostles,* Ellen White collapses these in *one* quality, namely "love."[4] In expanding on her point, she first shows why, before Jesus left the earth, He spent so much time with Peter and asked, "Do you love Me?" When Peter answered once, Jesus asked again and again, "Do you love Me?" The third time when Jesus asked, as we know from the scriptural record, Peter cried. Ellen White wrote, "Christ mentioned to Peter only one condition of service—'Lovest thou Me?' This is the essential qualification. Though Peter might possess every other, yet without the love of Christ he could not be a faithful shepherd over the flock of God. Knowledge, benevolence, eloquence, zeal—all are essential in the good work; but without the love of Christ in the heart, the work of the Christian minister is a failure."[5]

The previous comment we consider as vital because in today's fast-paced technological culture, our pastoral training would seem far from the pastoral life in which personages such as Abraham, Isaac, Jacob and his sons, David, and prophets like Amos honed their character and skills. For instance, when David wrote the twenty-third psalm and made his multiple other references throughout the Psalms to the loving-kindness of the Shepherd, he was writing from a firsthand caring-for-sheep experience. When Isaiah, Jeremiah, Ezekiel, Zechariah, Zephaniah, Nahum, Jude, and the other prophets and apostles spoke of the "brutal" and "reckless" ways in which the (so-called) shepherds were treating the sheep of God's flock, they spoke with a firsthand knowledge of what it meant to care for sheep.

They knew sheep, like the little boy in math class who shocked the teacher. When the teacher asked the class, "If a person has one hundred sheep and one leaves, how many are left?" All the students in the class except one little boy answered, "Ninety-nine, teacher." But the little boy kept insisting that none were left. "Well," asked the teacher, "could you explain to the class what you mean by none?" The little boy responded simply, "Well, teacher, you know math, but I know sheep—if one leaves, all leave."

What does this have to say about love? In our high-tech, microwave, cyberspace age, it is easy to become, as Charles R. Swindoll argues in another context, distant, untouched, and untouchable, uncaring and preoccupied with our own agendas so that we are unmoved by what is happening all around us.[6]

The actions of the shepherd

In leading away from the question as to who a pastor is and onto what a pastor is expected to do as nurturer, we have isolated some interesting issues.

1. The caregiver—dealing with hurting sheep. For example, everywhere that we have had the opportunity to minister, we have found people who are hurting and discouraged. Many have broken dreams and we can sense a note of hopelessness. Life often creates entanglements, and it would seem that everyone's susceptible to pain at one time or another. Because of the proclivity to make excuse for one's shortcomings, accommodating pain and despair becomes easier. The shepherd responds to hurting sheep, not with looks of sarcasm or words of condemnation and frustration, but with compassion and pity. This compassion includes having the ability and love to feel the pain of others and to be concerned about their predicament.

The world is desperate to experience the love and compassion of God as demonstrated in the life and ministry of His undershepherds. We are reminded in 1 John 3:17 that "If anyone has material possessions and sees his brother in need but has no pity on him, how can the love of God be in him?" (NIV). God's Word implies that we have a heart of compassion—the question is whether it is closed or open. The shepherd's heart is open to the sheep when they take the time to make a difference in their lives by encouraging them and by listening attentively to them. Good shepherds always look for sheep that they can bless. Shepherds don't mind being interrupted and inconvenienced if it means their interaction with the sheep brings relief and comfort.

Whenever we think of the pastoral ministry of Jesus, we reflect on the way He dealt with hurting sheep. A classic example of His compassion can be found in John 8:1–11 where Jesus did not condemn a woman caught in adultery but liberated her from the scorns of her accusers and certain death. He forgave her and encouraged her to go in peace and sin no more. In the Bible, Jesus always takes the side of the downtrodden and outcast. Whenever a member falls, a good shepherd will make certain they are not destroyed by other sheep. Like Jesus, the Chief Shepherd, the One who is our Model in all things pure and true, we must identify with the hurting and discouraged masses of humanity who find themselves lonely and discouraged in a sometimes hostile and friendless world. The prophetess to the remnant church reminds us that, "Christ's method alone will give true success in reaching the people. The Saviour mingled with men as one who desired their good. He showed His sympathy for them, ministered to their needs, and won their confidence."[7]

When we study the life of Jesus, we discover that He always took time for people. More than the shepherd's advice, more than their instruction, people need the shepherd's listening ear. The shepherd also understands the need, mentoring the flock with patience as he or she equips them to make prudent and life-enhancing decisions.

A reality that cannot be denied in this context is that sheep sometimes repeat the same mistakes, and it will require patience from the shepherd to continue to minister to the erring sheep—a patience that endures. The shepherd must therefore accept the role of nurturer and shepherd.

2. Leading the sheep to discern the leading of the Spirit in their lives. We note further the significance of leading the sheep to discern the leading of the Spirit in their lives. The author of Acts clearly admonishes all who aspire to oversee the flock of Christ to encourage those who are led to receive the Spirit. For those occupying even subordinate positions in the early church, the preeminent qualification was that they be persons "full of the Holy Spirit." It is, therefore, virtually impossible for pastors to guide their sheep in discerning the voice of God if they are not hearing that voice in a consistent way.

Leaders who have significantly influenced and advanced the cause of Christ were themselves Spirit-filled. Jesus Christ commanded His disciples to tarry in Jerusalem until they were endued with power from on high. The record says that "God anointed Jesus of Nazareth with the Holy Spirit and power" (Acts 10:38, NIV). The apostle Paul encouraged the leaders at Ephesus to " 'Keep watch over yourselves and all the flock of which the Holy Spirit has made you overseers' " (Acts 20:28, NIV).

As overseer, the shepherd teaches the flock to discern the will of God through the Christian disciplines of Bible study, prayer, worship, and fellowship with the believers. The flock needs to recognize the voice of God as He speaks to us in the twenty-first century, and be cognizant of the fact that there are many divergent voices that call out daily to the sheep for allegiance. In this context, shepherds are required to be most vigilant. God still speaks eloquently through His Holy Spirit in these times, and His Spirit never contradicts His Holy Word.

Prayer becomes a viable and powerful medium in the hand of Christians as they seek to discover God's will for their lives. Through prayer, we are able to listen more intently to the voice of the Holy Spirit as He leads us into all truth and comforts and guides us in our pursuit of the sanctified life. Paul says in 2 Corinthians 3:18, "But we all, with open face beholding as in a glass the glory of the Lord, are changed into the same image from glory to glory, even as by the Spirit of the Lord" (KJV).

This change means that you and I can share the glory of Christ and go from glory to glory through the Spirit of God.

3. Helping the sheep through their wilderness experiences. As good shepherds, pastors also have the responsibility to accompany their sheep when the sheep go out to pasture. The shepherd's task includes providing green grass, still waters, and being accountable for all the sheep. With plenty of food and water, sheep will lie still. However, the hungry sheep will become restless and prone to wandering in search of anything edible. Shepherds are not surprised when wandering sheep are hurt or lost. The shepherd must be diligent in the search for nutritious food for their flock, and fully aware of any hungry or wayward sheep that seek to stray.

In pastoral care, a major benefit of having contented sheep is the opportunity it provides for the shepherd to spend time in earnest communication with God. The shepherd can spend time with the Word, talk to God, rest, be rejuvenated, and spend quality time in recreation.

The shepherd must always be alert and ready, however, because discontented sheep are always present. Discontentment leads to wandering and lostness, resulting in pain and hurt. Thus, the task of feeding the sheep becomes even more imperative.

The biblical counsel very clearly relates to stray and lost sheep by emphasizing that the pastor must find them. In the words of Jesus, " 'If a man owns a hundred sheep, and one of them wanders away, will he not leave the ninety-nine on the hills and go to look for the one that wandered off?' " (Matthew 18:12, NIV). Obviously then, the care of every sheep must be the preoccupation of the shepherd, and thus the pastor must be accountable for every member.

The experience of Jesus and the Samaritan woman at the well should bring comfort to the pastor/shepherd (John 4:4–42). When she understood the importance of the water that Jesus offered, she exclaimed, " 'Sir, give me this water so that I won't get thirsty and have to keep coming here to draw water' " (verse 15, NIV). The pastor's intent should be to provide spiritual water for the sheep so they will feel no desire to drink from another stream. No wonder Jesus, the Great Shepherd, declared on the last day of the great feast, " 'If anyone is thirsty, let him come to me and drink. Whoever believes in me, as the Scripture has said, streams of living water will flow from within him' " (John 7:37, 38, NIV).

Sheep are extremely dependable animals. The shepherd must provide complete care for their sheep. During these intimate periods, the shepherd can initiate a special bonding, as guidance, direction, and communication takes place. Sheep will stray at times, and when they do, the hireling may not be concerned. But the pastor/shepherd cannot be comfortable until all the sheep are in the fold. Similarly, God holds the pastor accountable to God for every sheep in the fold.

4. Mediating fighting sheep. Multiple struggles and conflicts exist in a flock or community, even the one called church, and this is an unfortunate reality. However, it is to be understood that relationships are formed in conflict.[8] As with a flock, some persons and families always seem to be in conflict, and they find reasons to create and escalate divisions. Even Jesus had to deal with conflicts among His twelve disciples. The disciples were really angry at two of the brothers, James and John, for asking for seats on Jesus' right and left hands with the arguments even carried to the upper room. Jesus had to take time in that room to demonstrate that a community cannot survive where constant conflict exists (John 13). Later Jesus spent much time in prayer asking His Father to bring resolution to the problems among His disciples (John 17).

On one occasion in His ministry when Jesus was asked to resolve a certain conflict concerning the division of property among brothers, He responded resolutely, " 'Man, who appointed me a judge or an arbiter between you?' " (Luke 12:14, NIV). While pastors have a great responsibility in the resolution of conflicts, they are not to make this take all of their time. Pastors must make clear to the flock that living in disagreements will suck the vibrancy of the flock. At no time can conflict be trivialized. Therefore, pastors must identify the basis of a conflict, establish the significance of the conflict that needs to be brought to resolution, note the impact of the conflict on those involved in the conflict, and note the affect on the flock or total congregation. Then pastors should follow the scriptural principles that are effective in resolving the conflict. Working person-to-person resolves arguments in the best way, with the leadership of the church assisting.

Most importantly, in the effort to resolve conflicts, pastors must use intercessory prayers. Present the names of those in private and when possible, let them know that you are remembering them in prayer. While all pastors cannot be expected to have degrees in conflict management, all need to know that their flock will not grow if they do not find ways to resolve conflicts.

5. *Using the rod of correction.* As we reflect on the pastor as shepherd, the rod and the staff illustration connects well with our discussion on conflict resolution among the sheep. Both the rod and staff bring to mind what Kevin Leman and William Pentak observe in a chapter of their book *The Way of the Shepherd,* namely that the rod functions for protection, correction, and inspection.[9] One who has no clear understanding of the constitution of pastoral work will always view with a negative eye the work of the rod of protection, correction, and inspection. However, when one sees the interrelationship between the protection, the correction and the inspection becomes clear. As has been pointed out by Leman and Pentak, sometimes one needs to protect the sheep from intruders. Conflict does not always come from inside the flock, but often is brought by agents from outside. The flock thus needs to be protected from such outside agents that have come in to ravage the flock.[10] This means that pastors should not be afraid to get between their sheep and the wolves that are seeking to destroy their sheep.

Of course, destructive agents do not always come into the flock, but they wait for the sheep to become errant and isolated—considered the best way for the negative agent to attack the sheep. With the duty of the shepherd to correct the course of the sheep, the sheep can keep focused on the real goal. Because correction is not easy to do nor easy to take, the shepherd needs to have love that is deep enough, courage that is strong enough, and trust that is intense enough to bring about the correction. People, like sheep, go off course; they like to have their own way (Isaiah 53) and soon they may fall off rocks into ditches that are sometimes ravaged by wild animals or destroyed by some other agents that lay waiting for them. In bringing about correction, the pastor should take time to point out to the sheep or person(s) that what is intended does not include destruction or punishment of their souls, but instruction and re-demption.

The other significant and identified use of the rod, which should not be forgotten, is that of inspection. The shepherd who understands sheep knows the need for inspection of the sheep from time to time. Whether the shepherd stands at the door of the fold, or sits on a rock, or postured in another way in other places, shepherds needs to find out how their sheep are getting along. Ask them in the most respectful way, "How are things going?" It may be put as a general question or directed toward their faith, or health, or well-being. Leo Buscaglia, the professor who taught a course on love at the University of California, used to say to his students, "Let me tell you a little about me. You tell me a little about you." His claim was that his vulnerability caused his students to become vulnerable. Most times, he was able to develop a conversation from which he, as well as his students, benefited.

Yes, much can be said for the use of the rod of correction within contemporary church communities with all of the philosophies of independence, relativism, and diversity that are being tossed about. However, our communities need to be protected from brokenness, constrained from missteps, and protected from pests. The shepherd carries this burden and his or her effectiveness depends on the grace of God to carry it forward.

6. The pastor interceding for the sheep. Pastors, as shepherds, need to practice the ministry of intercession for themselves and their sheep. The biblical examples are many, but we can isolate Abraham, Jacob, Moses, and Jesus, since we named them among the exemplary shepherds. Abraham pleaded for Sodom and renewed his prayer until he had to say to God, "Oh let not the LORD be angry" (Genesis 18:30, KJV). He kept on interceding until he learned how far he could go with God. Then he rested in God's will and for his sake, Lot was saved. As the text says, "[God] remembered Abraham and brought Lot out of the catastrophe" (Genesis 19:29, NIV). Jacob wrestled with God on the night he feared to meet Esau. At the touch of dawn, he became an overcomer with God and was blessed and given a new name (Genesis 28). When Israel had made the golden calf we are told that "Moses went back to the Lord and said, 'Oh, what a great sin these people have committed! They have made themselves gods of gold. But now, please forgive their sin—but if not, then blot me out of the book that you have written' " (Exodus 32:31, 32, NIV). God heard him and offered to send an angel to go with Israel. Not satisfied, Moses went back to God and would not stop praying until God offered to go Himself with Israel, " 'I will do the very thing you have asked' " (Exodus 33:17, NIV). In the end, God showed Moses His back part as a token of His presence (verse 18).

The most memorable among the intercessors we are naming, though, is Jesus. As John records it, He prayed for Himself, His disciples, all who accept Him to the end of time, and for the unity of the church. He prayed and was assured of the Father's will. He prayed until He sweated blood (John 17). This prayer was long and intense. And like the others prayers we have named, this one prevailed. In the end, God sent angels to strengthen Jesus so that He went to the cross with assurance of protection.

In effect, true shepherding includes a ministry of intense intercession calling for prayers for oneself, prayers for one's flock in the fold, and prayers for the lost sheep. In such prayers, one should include the passion to be faithful in the work, the perspective concerning the kingdom, the patience to deal with struggling sheep, humility, tact, affection, tenderheartedness, tolerance, the Holy Spirit, wisdom, understanding, discernment, hope, and all the graces that are needed by the sheep and the shepherd. As shepherds, we must pray persistently and consistently, for only thus can our ministry be effective. As the prophet says, "I have posted watchmen on your walls, O Jerusalem; / they will never be silent day or night. / You who call on the Lord, / give yourselves no rest" (Isaiah 62:6, NIV).

---

1. Cf. Song of Solomon 1:8; Jeremiah 23:1, 2, 4; 50:6; Ezekiel 34:8; 1 Corinthians 9:7; 1 Peter 5:2; Jude 12.

2. Kenneth Gangel, *Feeding and Leading* (Grand Rapids, MI: Baker Book House, 1996). One might say that Dr. Gangel has placed "the cart before the horse" or that he

"puts the carrot before the stick," but that is not the criticism to be brought right now. A more important point is that he senses that the weight of the pastor as shepherd rests on two stones, namely leading and feeding.

3. See Jeremiah 3:15, also Dr. Ángel Rodríguez's brilliant chapter on "The Pastor and Theology" in this book.

4. Ellen G. White, *The Acts of the Apostles,* 515.

5. Ibid.

6. Charles Swindoll, *Hope Again: When Life Hurts and Dreams Fade* (Dallas, TX: Word Publishing, 1996), 124.

7. Ellen G. White, *The Ministry of Healing,* 143.

8. In her book, *Congregations in Conflict: Cultural Models of Local Religious Life* (New York: Cambridge University Press, 1999), Penny Edgell Becker supports our point with her study of several congregations of varied denominations in Chicago, where she found some highly structured ritual relationships amidst conflict. There are common things that hold people together and things that tend to drive them apart.

9. Kevin Leman and William Pentak, *The Way of the Shepherd: Seven Ancient Secrets to Managing Productive People* (Grand Rapids, MI: Zondervan, 2004), chap. 6.

10. One of the interesting observations about reading the New Testament epistles such as Galatians, 1 and 2 Timothy, Thessalonians, Jude, and Peter, is to see how much attention is given to guarding the churches against false shepherds. The apostles warned the churches to look out for them and to get rid of them out of the flock.

Chapter 17

The Pastor and Finances

Nikolaus Satelmajer with input from

Paul Douglas, Karnik Doukmetzian, Robert

Kyte, and Juan R. Prestol

Church members generally realize that the pastor's primary role envelopes spiritual responsibilities—preaching, teaching, evangelizing, visiting, and other types of ministry. A minister's real life, however, shows that the pastor performs this role in a world not always focused entirely on the spiritual. With that description of the reality of ministry, the pastor must not only be aware of but must also participate in functions different than the primary spiritual role of ministry.

In broad terms, these functions may be classified as the business of church operations. Within this area we will place finances, church property management, risk management, and other operational functions. As you consider this important topic of ministry, you will find helpful material in several books already available, but this chapter will focus more on the application of the policies, principles, and procedures stated in these sources.[1]

Finances

With finances recognized as a spiritually important part of church operations, a congregation that handles its finances responsibly will be more effective in carrying out the mission of sharing God with the world. Pastors, as an inspiration to their congregations, will thankfully follow Paul's advice: "But just as you excel in everything—in faith, in speech, in

180

knowledge, in complete earnestness and in your love for us—see that you also excel in this grace of giving" (2 Corinthians 8:7, NIV).

Seventh-day Adventist congregations have an established and tested financial system that has served and blessed the church well, and for this we express gratitude to our heavenly Father. We will review this system with the hope that you will see each section as an effective tool for church operations.

Inspiring their congregations to give according to the biblical model should be considered an important part of church finances. As Isaiah recorded, "unto us a Son is given," and Christ proclaimed, "This is My body, given for you," the model for giving came with our Savior's birth and His death. By encouraging the sharing of the gifts received joyfully as unworthy sinners, congregations could be led to internalize Paul's instruction, "Each man should give what he has decided in his heart to give, not reluctantly or under compulsion, for God loves a cheerful giver" (2 Corinthians 9:7, NIV). Giving back to our heavenly Example with gratitude for the blessings given to us as congregations would change the financial standard of every church.

Control of finances. Church finances should not be controlled by any one individual (pastor, treasurer, elder, for instance), but administered by individuals with an assigned authority. The church in business session has final authority for finances, and the church board within the authority given it by the church in business meetings oversees the finances. For example, the church treasurer prepares the church budget with input from other church leaders. With the budget reviewed by the church board, final approval comes at a subsequent church business meeting, and all church members in good and regular standing may vote. Churches that do not follow this process for financial preparation can easily find themselves in dispute over finances, with serious conflicts often developing.

When a budget has been voted, various church departments should have the opportunity to make expenditures without the church board having to approve each purchase. However, the church treasurer must recommend to the various departmental leaders that they do not spend all of their funds in the early part of the fiscal year and then have little or nothing left for the last part of the year.

Internal controls. Because the monies collected should be considered God's property, a church should adopt internal controls to make certain that finances are handled responsibly and to avoid both the possibility and the reality of the mishandling of funds. While the system may need to be different in a small church as compared to a very large congregation, the principles will apply in all situations.

Internal controls begin with the methods used for receiving tithes and offerings. After the offering has been collected, several individuals should take responsibility for securing it. If anything happens to the offering or if anyone raises questions as to how it has been handled, the issues may be resolved more effectively if several individuals had responsibility for the safety of the funds. In fact, it would be good if the same group did not always have this responsibility nor be close family members. Outlining a process for the handling of offerings, with the church board voting on the proposal before any problems occurred, would prove helpful. A good system will serve the church and will make the work easier for those responsible.

Another aspect of internal control has to do with the recognition of the importance of having a clear outline and quality system for disbursing funds. In all countries, all disbursements (checks, cash, or other banking instruments) should be properly authorized and needed documents in place, such as invoices or other similar backup documents.

Church treasurer. Because church treasurers perform a vital role in the church and have a very demanding responsibility, they spend more time doing their work than most members assume.

Pastors need to recognize the importance of this role and acknowledge the work of the treasurer before the church board as well as the church body. An occasional special praise time in song and word for the privilege of giving to the Lord (and occasionally incorporating an acknowledgment of the dedication and service of the treasurer) could also inspire the congregation. The vast majority of church treasurers in the Seventh-day Adventist Church are faithful and perform their work responsibly.

To help the treasurers stay faithful, pastors can do several things. For example, whenever the treasurer submits the monthly remittance of tithes and conference offerings to the conference, the pastor should receive a copy and spend some time reviewing it, noticing if there are any unusual developments. Should you see a large decrease or increase in tithe, ask the treasurer to give you insight as to what might have happened. (This is also true for any accounts.)

Thank the treasurer for the explanation and discuss whether or not you should talk with the board about some of the major financial trends. Even though there may be very logical reasons for the changes, the board should be kept informed. You could also show interest in the treasurer's work by discussing the monthly report with them. If the reports come in several months late consistently, the pastor and the board should consider this a serious problem. Late reports often signal that something inappropriate could be happening. And finally, encourage your treasurer to attend any training program offered by the conference.

One more thing needs to be recognized: since treasurers cannot create funds, the pastor and the church board need to respect the voted budget by not pressuring the treasurer to spend funds that do not exist.

Financial reports. The church board should receive a financial report from the treasurer, but reports should also be given to the whole congregation in an attitude of praise to God for the generosity of each person. After all, the funds come from the members, and we should speak to them about their privilege to give to the Lord when we need them to be more generous. Some churches publish, on a monthly basis, an abbreviated financial statement of the church, including a list of income and expenses and the balances of various funds. Members like to be informed and reports will create a sense of openness to instill members with more confidence in the church leadership. And by all means, thank God and the members for their support.

Church budgets. Every church needs to have a budget, and in order for finances to not become a major point of contention in the congregation, the church treasurer should not be the only one who prepares the budget. By coordinating the budget preparation, various ministries and departments of the church become involved. If they are simply told how much they can spend, without any input, those individuals will not be strong supporters of church finances. After the collection of the information from the various ministries and departments, the church board then needs to consider the proposals and make a recommendation about the budget to the entire church in business session. By presenting the privilege of giving to God as an honor, and as a result more individuals become involved, the larger the support base will be. Remember the budget as a reasonable plan, but circumstances may make it necessary to revisit the budget during the year. Again, a variety of individuals need to be involved in the review process.

Debt. Except for approved building projects, churches should avoid debt. Debt can become a hard-to-bear burden on a congregation and often becomes a point of major conflict in a church. Some members will argue that it's acceptable to incur debt because "the Lord will provide." If the Lord will provide, and He does, then He can also provide without the church incurring any debt. Once a congregation has incurred a debt for operating expenses, raising the funds needed to pay it off becomes very difficult. Members like to give for projects, ministries, and specific needs, but not for the eradication of debt.

If you are assigned to a congregation that has an operational debt, address the issue with the church board within a reasonable time frame, and make specific plans for getting out of debt. At that point, determining who is responsible for the situation would not represent good management. One approach would be to invite all members of the church board to agree that they will participate in the elimination of the debt, while encouraging each one to decide, with the guidance of their Lord, just how much they will contribute. Once you have that commitment, share that amount with the congregation as you thank the Lord for the dedication of the leadership of the church. Once members realize that their leaders have made a personal commitment to eliminate a debt, they will most likely follow. Ask the members to likewise make a commitment to pay off the debt and keep reporting to the congregation until the date of the elimination. Then have a special program to thank the Lord for His blessing and to thank the members for their participation.

Separation of funds. Church members give a variety of funds to the local church—tithe, local church offerings, conference offerings, and special offerings, for example. Be sure that the wishes of the donors are fulfilled. In our denominational system, tithe is remitted to the conference and no board or church leader has the authority to use it for other purposes. Offerings must be used as they have been designated. Whenever individuals, committees, or boards do not use the funds as designated, they are not being faithful in their duties. Proper use of funds builds confidence among the church members.

Do it in a timely manner. All financial reports should be prepared and presented in a timely manner. However, if an unavoidable delay occurs, tell the board and members the reason. If the church treasurer cannot complete the work in a timely manner, either additional help should be provided or in the case that the treasurer needs additional training, the conference should be notified. Late reports often create an atmosphere of distrust.

Auditing[2]

The Seventh-day Adventist Church uses a comprehensive and established auditing system that calls for the audit of the financial records of all denominational organizations (local conference, union conferences, General Conference, schools, and other church organizations). Likewise, the books kept by the treasurer of a congregation must be audited, as this creates confidence among the church members. After all, we must never forget that members have voluntarily joined the Seventh-day Adventist Church and that donations made by members should not be considered payments but gifts. After an audit, a report is usually presented, and that report needs to be shared with the entire board.

Church property

In our denomination, local church property is held in trust by the legal body (corporation, association, or similar body) set up by the local conference, and this system has worked well for the denomination. In this system, the local congregation decides, for example, if they wish to sell the church property. Such decisions are recommended by the church board, and then the church in business session votes upon that recommendation. Thus, no one individual or small group of individuals controls church property. Once the church in business session makes the decision, then the conference legal body takes action. Throughout the process, conference leaders should be consulted and invited to provide input. This comprehensive approach safeguards the disposition of church property with a similar approach used for the purchase of property and for building projects.

The legal process of buying or selling property or erection of buildings varies from country to country, and often even within a country the laws may vary from one area to another. Therefore, local leaders (pastors, elders, treasurers, etc.) should not sign any documents unless specifically asked to do so by the conference. If this process is not carefully followed, there may be serious consequences to the local leaders (as individuals or as a group) or to the local congregation. When in doubt, seek the counsel of the conference leaders.

Insurance and risk management

The denomination takes a very practical approach to insurance, with insurance protecting the denomination or providing for replacement of property in case of fire or other disasters. Working with the conference and Adventist Risk Management[3] (if it provides a service in your area) to determine the kind of insurance needed should be considered very important. Insurance laws vary from area to area and the local conference and Adventist Risk Management must contact proper organizations for insurance. Occasionally, insurance agencies that do not have experience with church organizations offer insurance (sometimes even at a lower cost), but only when the insurance is needed following a disaster does the congregation find out that they did not have proper or adequate coverage. Just because a church board member knows a good insurance agent and recommends that agent does not mean that the agent has an adequate policy that will handle church insurance.

Risk Management answers the question: how do you reduce the risk of loss, lawsuit, or injury? The church can reduce risk by keeping the facility repaired, clean, and have any hazards removed. A well-kept facility will be more appealing to members and visitors as well as minimize accidents.

Legal

The Seventh-day Adventist Church ministers in more than two hundred countries—almost every country in the world. With that being so, our denomination also operates in many legal systems. Local congregations need to be aware of the complexity of legal matters and the importance of operating in such a manner so that unnecessary legal problems do not develop. Again, the congregational leadership should consult with conference leaders who have access to appropriate legal counsel when legal matters surface.

---

1. See the *Seventh-day Adventist Church Manual* (Silver Spring, MD: Secretariat General Conference of Seventh-day Adventists, 2005); *Seventh-day Adventist Minister's Handbook* (Silver Spring, MD: General Conference Ministerial Association, 1995), with a new edition to be released in 2009; and *Pastoral Ministry* (Silver Spring, MD: General Conference Ministerial Association, 1995).

2. See www.gcasconnect.org.

3. See www.adventistrisk.org.

Chapter 18

The Pastor and Multichurch Districts

Pardon K. Mwansa

The challenges of pastoring multichurches includes the fact that ministers do not have enough time to carry out all the duties that demand their attention. In addition, they have other things that need attention apart from pastoring churches.

My first pastoral assignment consisted of three churches with a membership of over seven hundred in each group and four companies with a membership of at least fifty people in each group. The total membership in the district was about twenty-three hundred.

On my first Sabbath in the district, I preached at one of these three churches, and then in the afternoon raced to conduct a Bible study at the second church. At the end of that Bible study, I found elders from the third church waiting for me to arrange for the baptism at their church. As if this was not enough, that same week, a well-known church member became ill, and I went to visit him. After a few days, he died, and the church asked me to conduct the funeral service, which I gladly did. However, now others wanted me to conduct *their* funeral services, and we had at least one funeral somewhere in the district almost every week. As if this was not enough, I had just married that year.

How do pastors care for many churches successfully and still do all the other things that are expected of them—things such as being a spouse and/or a parent? What I have shared in this chapter covers what I did when I served as a pastor of many churches, and what I have learned during my other years of serving God.

In spite of the challenges that come with caring for more than one church, I discovered that if planned well, pastoring many churches can be enjoyable. Admittedly, by the time I was transferred from that district, I loved my work so much that I had a hard time leaving, and, from the messages conveyed by the members, I think they were sorry to see me go.

Multichurch district pastoring may mean different things for different people. For the pastor in the Democratic Republic of Congo, it may mean caring for as many as twenty organized churches with a total membership of eight thousand. And they do not have transportation to reach half of them in one year, even if they wanted to do so. On the other hand, some pastors may have two or three churches. Whatever the situation, the principles shared below are very applicable to all. I have therefore defined multichurch pastoring as simply caring for more than one church.

A biblical model

There are three key biblical passages used to build the kind of model that I have written about: Exodus 18:17–23; Numbers 11:10–17; and Acts 6:1–6. All of these passages deal with principles that one could use when pastoring many churches.

1. The setting of the first one. Moses' father in-law, Jethro, was visiting Moses when he noticed that Moses "took his seat to serve as judge for the people, and they stood around him from morning till evening" (Exodus 18:13, NIV). When Jethro saw this, he gave Moses this counsel taken from Exodus 18:14–23:

> **Jethro:** "What is this you are doing for the people? Why do you alone sit as judge, while all these people stand around you from morning till evening?"

> **Moses:** "Because the people come to me to seek God's will. Whenever they have a dispute, it is brought to me, and I decide between the parties and inform them of God's decrees and laws."

Jethro: "What you are doing is not good. You and these people who come to you will only wear yourselves out. The work is too heavy for you; you cannot handle it alone. Listen now to me and I will give you some advice, and may God be with you. You must be the people's representative before God and bring their disputes to him. Teach them the decrees and laws, and show them the way to live and the duties they are to perform. But select capable men from all the people—men who fear God, trustworthy men who hate dishonest gain—and appoint them as officials over thousands, hundreds, fifties and tens. Have them serve as judges for the people at all times, but have them bring every difficult case to you; the simple cases they can decide themselves. That will make your load lighter, because they will share it with you. If you do this and God so commands, you will be able to stand the strain, and all these people will go home satisfied" (NIV).

2. The setting of the second one. The second story and counsel of God comes from a situation that arose while Moses was leading the children of Israel, which is recorded in Numbers 11:10–17:

Moses heard the people of every family wailing, each at the entrance to his tent. The LORD became exceedingly angry, and Moses was troubled.

Moses: "[Lord,] why have you brought this trouble on your servant? What have I done to displease you that you put the burden of all these people on me? Did I conceive all these people? Did I give them birth? Why do you tell me to carry them in my arms, as a nurse carries an infant, to the land you promised on oath to their forefathers? Where can I get meat for all these people? They keep wailing to me, 'Give us meat to eat!' I cannot carry all these people by myself; the burden is too heavy for me. If this is how you are going to treat me, put me to death right now—if I have found favor in your eyes—and do not let me face my own ruin."

The Lord: "Bring me seventy of Israel's elders who are known to you as leaders and officials among the people. Have them come to the Tent of Meeting, that they may stand there with you. I will come down and speak with you there, and I will take of the Spirit that is on you and put the Spirit on them. They will help you carry the burden of the people so that you will not have to carry it alone" (NIV; italics supplied).

3. The setting of the third one. The third passage comes from Acts 6:1–6, when the people who were being led by the apostles brought a complaint to them:

> *In those days when the number of disciples was increasing, the Grecian Jews among them complained against the Hebraic Jews because their widows were being overlooked in the daily distribution of food.*
>
> **So the Twelve gathered all the disciples together and said,** "It would not be right for us to neglect the ministry of the word of God in order to wait on tables. Brothers, choose seven men from among you who are known to be full of the Spirit and wisdom. We will turn this responsibility over to them and will give our attention to prayer and the ministry of the word."
>
> *This proposal pleased the whole group. They chose Stephen, a man full of faith and of the Holy Spirit; also Philip, Procorus, Nicanor, Timon, Parmenas, and Nicolas from Antioch, a convert to Judaism. They presented these men to the apostles, who prayed and laid their hands on them* (NIV; italics supplied).

Listed below are the main points relevant to multichurch pastoring:

1. God has not called one or just a few people to do everything required in caring for the needs of the spiritual family of God.
2. If one person or a few people try to do everything involved in caring for people, they will not be able to stand the strain and

could be ruined as a result. Also, the people they are leading may not be happy because of unsatisfactory services.

3. God would like leaders responsible for many people to delegate some of the work to others so that by themselves, they will not do all the work.

4. Care must be taken in selecting those people that will help in the caring for the work and the family of God. Only trustworthy individuals filled with the Holy Spirit should be given such tasks.

5. Through the gift of the Holy Spirit, God will empower everyone who cares for the family of God with those gifts necessary to carry out the work successfully. The same Holy Spirit who enables the pastor to serve the church will enable other men and women selected for ministry to serve as well.

"Paul and Barnabas appointed elders for them in each church and, with prayer and fasting, committed them to the Lord, in whom they had put their trust" (Acts 14:23, NIV). Paul understood and taught that the Holy Spirit becomes the enabling power behind every person who ministers to others, be it a pastor or a local church elder. Speaking about elders, he said, "Keep watch over yourselves and all the flock of which the Holy Spirit has made you overseers. Be shepherds of the church of God, which he bought with his own blood" (Acts 20:28, NIV).

With these five points understood, we can now focus on how one person, the pastor, can face the challenges of pastoring more than one church.

Getting organized

For the pastor to become organized, the following steps are necessary:

1. Understand clearly who you are as you focus on the larger picture and your role expectations.
2. Allocate blocks of time to carry out the expectations of each role.

3. Develop a list, in consultation with the churches and the conference, of your mission and what the leaders expect you to do in the district for a healthy church life.

4. Determine your primary and secondary roles in the management of the churches in your district.

5. Delegate to responsible people the activities of the church and trust the Holy Spirit to give them success.

6. Develop and implement a teaching or training program for the people selected to help you run the church.

7. Establish a system for the development, implementation, and evaluation of the work in the district.

8. Learn to orchestrate the team that you are working with.

How do these fit into the bigger picture?

Understanding the larger picture and expected roles

A pastor can be defined as the following:

1. A person
2. A husband or wife
3. A father or mother
4. A leader of churches

The importance of knowing the many hats that you wear includes keeping the bigger picture of who you are and what you are expected to do in mind as you do ministry, lest you make ministry who *you* are. You are not ministry. You are a minister, among other things, and these may be equally important. In his article, "Multichurch District Life and Children," Richard Daly concludes that God calls ministers to be husbands and fathers before they are ministers.[1]

Allocate time to each of your roles

The implication of understanding who you are, if you will have a successful and balanced ministry and life, means that you will have to distribute your use of time among all the things that identify you. As a husband or wife, you will need time for your spouse; as a father or mother, time for your children; as a person, time to do exercise and attend to your personal needs, such as studying and praying; as a minister, time for duties at the church or visiting the church members, for instance.

You are one person and you have only twenty-four hours in a day, seven days in a week, and twelve months in a year. You can only do so much in one area. You have to share your time in a balanced manner.

1. Block time for yourself—for you personally. This is time when you study the Bible and pray to God for you first, the family, and the church family.

2. Block time for your family—that is, your wife and your children. Remember, if they are not with you, your ministry will not be successful.

3. Block time for your pastoral ministry in your district. By way of example, you may block out two hours in the morning for your study and prayer time; you may block out Wednesday as a family day, besides the time you will spend with your family every day; and you may schedule ministry in the afternoons and weekends. Many ministers testify that Sunday may not be a good family day because most meetings are held on that day.[2]

List what is expected to be done for the well-being of the district

The two major objectives for the work of any pastor are

1. to invite unsaved people into salvation and fellowship with the family of God;
2. to nurture those who have received salvation in Christ into spiritual maturity.

The minister will accomplish these two by doing many things, including the following:

1. Preaching
2. Training laity who are elected to serve into various offices

3. Visitations of members
4. Conducting evangelistic meetings
5. Planning for the work of the church or the district
6. Promoting various denominational programs
7. Chairing of meetings such as church or school boards, for instance
8. Conducting spiritual revival meetings or weeks of prayer
9. Promote, attend, and/or speak at camp meetings
10. Conduct ceremonies such as baptisms and weddings, for instance
11. Administration work such as ensuring finances are available for the smooth running of the churches, ensuring that reports to the conference are submitted, and other duties

Determine your primary and secondary roles

Frankly speaking, all the activities done to bring individuals into salvation and nurturing believers into spiritual maturity can be done by somebody else and done pretty well. Therefore, one of your goals as a pastor is to equip, by way of training, church members with the tools and motivation that will enable them to do ministry so well that they can run the church without you. Let us face it: if you have more than one church to pastor, you cannot preach in each of those churches every Sabbath. The same goes for all other activities. You now have to learn to trust that the same Holy Spirit who gives you messages and power to preach will work with others to do the same. You must decide what role you will play and the work you will do within that role.

Your primary responsibility will be that of a trainer and a manager. As a trainer, you will attempt to equip all the church officers by way of training them or scheduling training events through the conference or union. Training must be high on your responsibility list when you are caring for more than one church. Jesus called the Twelve Apostles because He needed to train them to do what He could not do after He was gone. There are certain areas of training that are a must.

1. Training identified people how to preach Sabbath sermons.
2. Training newly elected church officers how to carry out their duties, both the elders and those serving in departmental positions.

As a manager, you have to attempt to develop the skills needed for you to be on top of things—to know what is happening and have a system to respond to situations as need be. You are the pastor of the churches and as such, you are responsible for everything that happens in them. As manager, you basically facilitate others to do the work and ensure that they do what needs to be done.

A careful study of the *Church Manual* will show very clearly the functions of officers who are appointed to serve the church each given year.[3] Your job will be to

1. bring to the attention of each elected officer of a church what is expected of them in that role;
2. supply them with any needed resource materials for them to perform their jobs well;
3. train them in how to carry out their duties.

Decisions about the life and ministry of the church are made through the local church board. One of your duties will be to train local church board members to know what their rights, duties, limitations, etc., are as they function as church board members. You will also have to train your elders how to chair meetings successfully. Now, for all these things to be done, you need to establish a system of planning, implementing the plans, and evaluating the work that is done in the district. This leads us to the next section.

Establish a system of planning, implementing, and evaluating work

Three elements need to be addressed:

1. Who are the key people that you regularly need to help you run the church?

2. How often do you want to meet with those key people in order for you to be informed and to ensure work is being done?

3. When you meet with these people, what are the routine objectives that you need to accomplish at each of the meetings you have? For this to happen, you need a clear structure of how you will work.

A structure means a system through which you carry out your operations and also monitor the progress of your business. There are three types of meetings that I would propose:

1. Weekly meetings
2. Monthly meetings
3. Quarterly meetings

The weekly meetings may focus on church boards and such meetings when you need to be present. You will serve primarily as counselor at such meetings. The monthly meetings may involve your meeting with people who are helping you to preach. These gatherings would need to focus on the preaching done in your district, covering the areas that you as the pastor believe should be covered for the church to have a balanced life. If you were preparing a menu, you would not want your churches to be feeding on beans only; you want them to be fed with a balanced meal. If you do not plan the subjects to cover through sermons with those who help you preach, you may all be saying the same things and failing to be broad. Inspirational sermons should be included but a schedule for doctrinal and other kinds of sermons is also important. During these monthly meetings, you can discuss the subjects you would like to cover for particular months and also have prayer together with your preachers. This may be a meeting held only once a month.

The quarterly meetings would likely focus on planning and report sharing. Because you will do a lot of planning, you will need to have a District Planning and Evaluation Committee (DPEC). You can give it any name you want, as long as it does the work intended. At these district meetings, it would be profitable if each church was asked to report on the events of their church and also the future plans they have. This can serve as inspiration to other churches that may not be doing much. The following diagram gives an idea of how this may work.

	Weekly	Monthly	Quarterly
Target group	Church board members	Preachers and church elders	Elders and other key church leaders, such as treasurer, clerks, etc.
Objectives	To give counsel to local church board members during their board meetings	**Elders:** Reporting on baptisms Reporting on finances Church board decisions Other key activities of the church **Preachers:** Review of themes for sermons Pray together for power	Purpose of these quarterly meetings is to receive reports of activities, review future plans the church will engage in, pray together as a district team, be motivated for service, report on special events and activities, share the district accomplishments and summary report of all churches. Receive treasury reports on offerings, etc. Job descriptions discussed for different functions. Clear articulation of expectations from each church when a meeting is held.
Expectations	Well-conducted church board meetings	Empowered elders and preachers	A well-informed district: clear expectations, clear goals, united district with an informed agenda that everyone is aware of

Conclusion

While pastoring many churches can be a challenge, when good planning has gone into it, it can be done and done happily. The elements that need to be mastered in order to do a successful job include the following:

1. Understanding clearly the larger picture of who you are and the role expectations of each dimension of who you are.
2. Allocate blocks of time to carry out the expectations of each of those roles.
3. Develop a list, in consultation with the churches and the conference (mission), of what is expected to be done in the district for a healthy church life.
4. Determine your primary and secondary roles in the management of the churches in your district.
5. Delegate to responsible people the work of the church and trust the Holy Spirit to give them success.
6. Develop and implement a teaching or training program for the people you select to help you run the church.
7. Establish a system by which you are able to participate in the development, implementation, and evaluation of the work in the district.
8. Learn to orchestrate the team with whom you are working.

---

1. Richard Daly, "Multichurch District Life and Children," *Ministry,* August 2007.

2. Ibid., 7.

3. *Seventh-day Adventist Church Manual,* 17th ed. (Silver Spring, MD: Secretariat General Conference of Seventh-day Adventists, 2005).